USS Wisconsin (BB-64)
From World War II to the Persian Gulf to Museum Ship

DAVID DOYLE

SCHIFFER MILITARY
4880 Lower Valley Road Atglen, PA 19310

Copyright © 2020 by David Doyle

Library of Congress Control Number: 2020930688

All rights reserved. No part of this work may be reproduced or used in any form or by any means—graphic, electronic, or mechanical, including photocopying or information storage and retrieval systems—without written permission from the publisher.

The scanning, uploading, and distribution of this book or any part thereof via the Internet or any other means without the permission of the publisher is illegal and punishable by law. Please purchase only authorized editions and do not participate in or encourage the electronic piracy of copyrighted materials.

"Schiffer Military" and the arrow logo are trademarks of Schiffer Publishing, Ltd.

Designed by Justin Watkinson
Technical Layout by Jack Chappell
Type set in Impact/Minion Pro/Univers LT Std

ISBN: 978-0-7643-6013-8
Printed in China

Published by Schiffer Publishing, Ltd.
4880 Lower Valley Road
Atglen, PA 19310
Phone: (610) 593-1777; Fax: (610) 593-2002
E-mail: Info@schifferbooks.com
www.schifferbooks.com

For our complete selection of fine books on this and related subjects, please visit our website at www.schifferbooks.com. You may also write for a free catalog.

Schiffer Publishing's titles are available at special discounts for bulk purchases for sales promotions or premiums. Special editions, including personalized covers, corporate imprints, and excerpts, can be created in large quantities for special needs. For more information, contact the publisher.

We are always looking for people to write books on new and related subjects. If you have an idea for a book, please contact us at proposals@schifferbooks.com.

Acknowledgments

This book would not have been possible without the gracious help of many individuals and institutions. Beyond the invaluable help provided by Clayton Allen and the staff of the Nauticus, as well as the staff of the National Archives, I am indebted to Tom Kailbourn, Scott Taylor, Dana Bell, Tracy White, Rick Davis, Dave Baker, Roger Torgeson, Sean Hert, Robert Hanshew, Chris Hughes, and James Noblin. Especially helpful was Dominic Menta with the USS *Wisconsin* Association, who generously provided many scarce photos. Their generous and skillful assistance adds immensely to the quality of this volume. In addition to such wonderful friends and colleagues, the Lord has blessed me with a wonderful wife, Denise, who has tirelessly scanned thousands of photos and documents for this and numerous other books. Beyond that, she is my best friend, my partner, and an ongoing source of support and inspiration.

Contents

	Introduction	4
CHAPTER 1	Construction	6
CHAPTER 2	1940s Service	24
CHAPTER 3	1950s Service	62
CHAPTER 4	The Long Rest	94
CHAPTER 5	Return to Service	98
CHAPTER 6	Museum Ship	114

Introduction

The Iowa-class battleships were the pinnacle of US battleship construction. The aborted Montana-class battleships (BB 66–71) were to have been more heavily armed and armored but weren't planned to have the speed and maneuverability of the *Iowa*s.

Construction of six Iowa-class battleships was begun during World War II, but only four were completed. The other two, *Illinois* (BB-65) and *Kentucky* (BB-66), were never finished, making *Wisconsin* (BB-64) numerically the United States' last battleship.

Although *Wisconsin* was launched in Philadelphia on the same day (January 29, 1944) that its sister ship *Missouri* (BB-63) was launched in New York, laborers in Philadelphia completed *Wisconsin* first, and it was commissioned almost two months prior to *Missouri*.

The Iowa-class ships were conceived within the limitations of the London Naval Treaty.

Following World War I, a series of international treaties had been put in place limiting the number, size, and armament of warships to be operated by the signatories, which included most of the world powers. These early attempts at arms limitation treaties were moderately successful, with the naval architects of most signatories soon stretching the limit of the terms. In 1934, Japan gave formal notice that it was withdrawing from the treaties. Germany, by the way, was not involved in the naval treaties, since the Treaty of Versailles, which marked its capitulation in World War I, already placed significant prohibitions on Germany's armaments.

By March 1936, only the United States, Great Britain, and France were bound by any of the treaties. In March 1938, in view of shipbuilding activities worldwide, these nations invoked an escalator clause in the Second London Naval Treaty, which raised the maximum allowed capital ship displacement from 35,000 to 45,000 tons.

Warship design has always been a battle of desires versus practicality. Bigger guns increase displacement, as does heavier or more extensive armor protection. More speed requires larger machinery, which requires a larger hull to house it, and of course the machinery has to be protected by armor, which increases the weight. In order to maintain a given speed, more power is required, and the cycle starts again.

Under the initial clauses of the treaties, battleships were limited to 35,000 tons of displacement, and the North Carolina and South Dakota classes adhered to that. Armed with nine 16-inch, 45-caliber guns, the six ships of these two classes had top speeds of about 26 knots.

As early as 1923, the United States had considered the possibility that it would need to defend the Pacific against Japan. At such extreme distances from the US, the fleet would be extremely vulnerable to cruiser and aircraft carrier attacks, and many felt that fast, powerful battleships would be required to counter this threat.

In January 1938, Capt. A. J. Chantry, head of the Design Division of the Bureau of Construction and Repair, instituted a study of designs of 16-inch gunships that could be accommodated by the 110-foot-wide locks of the Panama Canal and were capable of making 35 knots.

As these studies and requirements were refined, the form of the American "fast battleship" came together, and on June 2, 1938, a proposal for a 33-knot, nine-gun, 44,559-ton vessel was presented to the Navy General Board. By Act of Congress on May 17, 1938, construction of two ships of the new design was authorized. Contracts for construction of two ships built to the new design were signed on July 1, 1939. The first ship of the new class, BB-61, would be the *Iowa*, namesake ship of the class.

All four of the Iowa-class battleships steamed together as Battleship Division 2 on June 7, 1954, off the Virginia Capes, with *Iowa* in the foreground and *Wisconsin* next to it, then *Missouri* and, in the distance, *New Jersey*. This was the only time all the *Iowa*s operated together. This photo captures the pinnacle of US Navy gunnery firepower. *National Archives*

CHAPTER 1
Construction

Construction of the *Wisconsin* began at the Philadelphia Navy Yard on January 25, 1941. The same yard also had begun the USS *New Jersey* (BB-62) and would begin the fifth Iowa-class battleship, BB-65, the *Illinois*, construction of which was canceled in August 1945 when *Illinois* was 22 percent complete.

In order to accommodate the hull of the massive battleships, the builder's ways at the shipyard had to be enlarged. Shipways 2 and 3 were lengthened by 325 feet, to 1,135 feet each, allowing *Wisconsin* to be constructed almost simultaneously alongside *New Jersey* (construction on *New Jersey* began in September 1940).

Unlike most prior battleships, the heavy armor plates forming the side belt armor were mounted internally, meaning that they had to be installed while the ship was on the ways. Likewise, the turbines and machinery were installed while on the ways, leading to a launching weight of 36,446 tons—one of the heaviest launching weights in the world—but still only a portion of its ultimate total weight.

Although begun only four months after *New Jersey*, *Wisconsin* was launched exactly twelve months after the Garden State battleship. This was in part due to other vessels having a higher construction priority.

The ship's sponsor, Madge Goodland, who smashed the bottle of champagne over the bow and christened the ship *Wisconsin*, was the wife of Wisconsin governor Walter Goodland. The launching date was the second anniversary of the Japanese attack on Pearl Harbor.

At the appointed time, the hull of *Wisconsin* slid down the ways, lubricated with 100,000 pounds of grease, into the Delaware River, slewing cables coupling the hull to mounds of anchor chain in an effort to slow the hull once it was waterborne. Tugboats quickly rectified this error, and the hull was moved to a drydock for removal of launching equipment and the machining of the turret roller paths. From there it was moved to Pier 4 for fitting out.

While the launch of a capital ship is a significant occasion, there is a great deal of work remaining to be done to transform a massive hull into a functioning ship. For example, in the case of *Wisconsin*, this involved installing 5,000 light fixtures, 14,000 valves, 2,990 telephones, and 84,480 feet of ventilation ducting and applying 156 tons of paint. When finally completed, 7,000 men had worked 2,891,334 man-days and had two casualties. The men used 4,300,000 feet of welding rod and had hammered home over one million rivets, all according to 174 pages of blueprints.

The fitting-out finally complete, on April 16, 1944, following remarks by RAdm. Milo Frederick Draemel, commandant of the Philadelphia Navy Yard, the ship was commissioned, becoming USS *Wisconsin*. Its first commanding officer, fittingly a Wisconsin native and veteran of service on the "old" *Wisconsin* (BB-9), was Capt. Earl Everett Stone.

The progress of work on the *Wisconsin* is viewed from off the starboard stern looking forward, on April 7, 1942. In the foreground, sections of the frames with plates of the shell—the outer skin of the hull—riveted to them are under construction in the bottom of the stern. Farther forward are lateral bulkheads of the engine rooms and firerooms of the machinery spaces. *National Archives*

The bottom of the bow is in the foreground of this view of the *Wisconsin* facing aft, on July 8, 1942. The barbette of turret 2 is a short distance to the front of the forward lateral bulkhead of the machinery spaces. Stacked to the front of the barbette are prefabricated units of frame sections with steel plates attached. *National Archives*

The ship is seen from off the stern on July 8, 1942. In the machinery spaces, the upper parts of the eight Babcock & Wilcox boilers are visible: specifically, the steam drums and the economizers. *National Archives*

In a view from above the stern of the *Wisconsin* on January 12, 1943, the machinery spaces between the barbettes for turrets 2 and 3 have been covered with deck. Three of the cylindrical, heavily armored barbettes for the 16-inch/50-caliber guns are under construction; in the foreground is the lower barbette for turret 3. *National Archives*

The scene in the preceding photo is viewed from a slightly different perspective. Returning to the lower barbette of turret 3 (*in the foreground*), the top of this structure is situated between where the main deck and the second deck will ultimately be, and consists of two concentric rings of armor, the inner ring being conical, narrower at the top than at the bottom. The top of the inner ring supported the roller track, on which rollers at the bottom of the turret structure moved. *National Archives*

Construction of the framing for the bow is underway in the foreground in this undated photo, quite possibly taken on the same date as the preceding photo, January 12, 1943. The shape of the bulbous bow is evident. Staging for the builders to work from is erected alongside most of the hull. *National Archives*

A little over a week before its launching, the *Wisconsin* is viewed from the front, showing the majestic sweep of its lines, including the bulbous bow. Atop the forecastle is a tub-shaped splinter shield for a 20 mm gun emplacement. The hole below the shield is the bullnose, for passing out a hawser. The port anchor is hanging by a cable from the port hawsepipe; anchor chains issuing from the hawsepipes are hanging from the sides of the forecastle. *National Archives*

The bow of the *Wisconsin* is viewed straight on, a short time before its launching. The starboard anchor has been hauled up alongside the bow. *National Archives*

The *Wisconsin* towers high above an administrative building at the Philadelphia Navy Yard a short time before its launching. The building ways were high above ground level at the point where the ship's bow was situated. Sufficient slope was designed into the building ways to allow gravity to let the ship slide rearward down the ways and into the water when launched. *National Archives*

In another view of the port bow of the *Wisconsin*, draft marks are visible on the bow below the port anchor, to provide information on the depth of the bottom of the hull, once launched. The ship took thirty million man hours to complete, at a cost of $110 million. *National Archives*

On December 7, 1943, two years to the day after the Japanese attack on Pearl Harbor, a crowd has gathered to witness the launching of the battleship *Wisconsin*. A temporary, white grid has been painted on the port side of the bow, apparently for visual reference concerning the attitude of the hull in the water after launching. The structure on the lower part of the hull is the bow poppet, a support cradle that also served as a bearing surface when the ship slid down the building ways. *National Archives*

The starboard side of the bow poppet is evident in this view. Shipyard workers, naval officers, and others are gathered on the deck of the battleship. Work on the superstructure had begun, including the smokestacks and the conning tower. A temporary cover encloses the upper part of the conning tower, at the front of the superstructure. The gun turrets are not installed; conical covers are over the wells of the barbettes. The twin 5-inch/38-caliber gun mounts are installed, but their armored shields are not present yet, so canvas covers are slung over the mounts. *National Archives*

CONSTRUCTION 13

The stern of the ship was fitted with poppets. The ones on the port side are seen between the port inboard and outboard propeller shafts. The poppets were removed after the launching. In the absence of the real propellers, which would be installed later, in drydock, small, dummy propellers are installed on the shafts. *National Archives*

The *Wisconsin* is observed from off its starboard stern on the day of its launching, December 7, 1943. On the stern are sponsons in which quadruple 40 mm antiaircraft gun mounts will later be installed. Attached to the hull were numerous draglines and slewing lines. The draglines were to slow down the momentum of the ship after it became waterborne, while the slewing lines were intended to make the ship turn more or less at right angles to the launching ways once it was waterborne. This was to prevent the ship from becoming beached on the opposite shore of the Delaware River. Enveloping the ship are the craneways for the overhead transverse cranes. *National Archives*

During the launching ceremony for the battleship *Wisconsin* on December 7, 1943, a naval officer addresses the audience immediately to the front of the bow. To his rear is seated the sponsor of the ship, Madge Goodland, whose husband, Wisconsin governor Walter S. Goodland, is standing behind the naval officer. *National Archives*

Madge Goodland, the sponsor of the battleship *Wisconsin*, is poised to smash the ceremonial bottle of champagne on the bow of the ship, to christen it, while her husband, Governor Walter S. Goodland, stands to her side. *National Archives*

Immediately following the christening of the *Wisconsin*, hydraulic triggers were actuated, releasing the ship to begin its slide down the well-greased ground ways, also called slipways. Before this event could occur, there was a carefully orchestrated procedure to shift the enormous mass of the ship from the keel blocks and shores, which supported the ship during construction, to the ways, which supported it during launching. *National Archives*

The stern has entered the water as the *Wisconsin* is being launched. Because of the size of the hull, four ground ways were used for the Iowa-class battleships; the outer ways were narrower than the inner ones. Since the bow was narrow, the outer ground ways extended only from amidships to the water. *National Archives*

Shortly after the *Wisconsin* has become fully waterborne after its launching, the port anchor has been dropped, causing a large splash along its bow. In these postlaunching photos, note how high the ship's bow is riding on the water, compared with the stern. *National Archives*

The *Wisconsin* has come to rest off the Philadelphia Navy Yard after dropping the port anchor. The state of construction of the superstructure is apparent. Scaffolding is present along the superstructure and the aft smokestack. A crowd of spectators are present on the wharf in the left background. *National Archives*

The *Wisconsin* is viewed from off its starboard stern shortly after the dropping of the port anchor. The ship is dressed fore and aft with flags and pennants. From here, the ship would be towed by tugboats to a fitting-out dock, where construction of the ship would continue during the ensuing four months. *National Archives*

A backlit battleship *Wisconsin* has lowered its port anchor after coming to rest upon launching. Jutting from the upper front of the superstructure is a temporary cover over the conning tower, the very heavily armored structure that housed the ship's navigating, command, and fire-control systems and personnel during battle. *National Archives*

CONSTRUCTION 17

The lower structure of turret 2 is resting on a concrete floor called the turret slab, at Philadelphia Navy Yard on December 22, 1943. The front of the structure is facing the camera. The top two levels are the upper projectile flat and the lower projectile flat. At the center of both projectile flats is a circular bulkhead, inside which was machinery. Connecting to the bottom of the lower projectile flat are powder and projectile hoists, on the bottom of which is the powder-handling platform. *National Archives*

On the turret slab on December 21, 1943, is the lower structure of turret 1, viewed from the front. Because of the lower position of turret 1 with reference to turret 2, the distance from the powder-handling platform, *at the bottom*, to the lower projectile flat is much shorter on this structure than on that seen in the preceding photo. *National Archives*

The lower structure of turret 1 is supported by a stand on the turret slab and is viewed from the rear. On the second-highest level, that of the lower projectile flat, the three projectile hoists are installed. On the bottom level, that of the powder-handling platform, to the right is the right powder-hoist trunk. At the center of that platform is the central column, with ladder rungs welded to it. Obscured by the scaffolding to the left are the center and left powder-hoist trunks, which were positioned together, with no space between them. *National Archives*

A sling weighing 12 tons and with a capacity of 150 gross tons, suspended from an overhead crane, is hooked to cables at the top of the lower structure of turret 2 and is just beginning to lift the structure from the turret slab, on December 22, 1943. *National Archives*

CONSTRUCTION 19

The lower structure of turret 2 is viewed from the front right as it is being carried by overhead crane from the turret slab to the battleship *Wisconsin* at its fitting-out dock, at the Philadelphia Navy Yard, on December 22, 1943. On the bottom level is the right powder-hoist trunk, with its loading doors, slightly tilted, at the bottom. On the far side of the lower level is the center powder hoist; the left powder hoist is on the opposite side of the center hoist and is not visible from this angle. *National Archives*

Before turret 2 was mounted on its barbette, this photo of the circular foundation of the turret, a cylinder slightly narrower in diameter at the top than at the bottom, was taken on December 21, 1943. The top of the circular foundation, covered here with planks to protect it from damage, formed the bottom roller track. Around the inner side of the top of the foundation is a stationary, annular rack. When the turret was completed, two electrohydraulically operated pinion gears engaged the annular rack in order to traverse the turret. Temporary staging is set up inside the well. *National Archives*

Taken two days after the preceding photo, this view of the well of turret 1 shows how the turret foundation, in the lower part of the photo, is situated with respect to the upper barbette, in the upper part of the photo. Workers are installing rollers on the lower roller track with the help of a jury rig. The rotating structure of the turret will rest on, and traverse on, these rollers. There were seventy-two rollers per turret, arranged in twelve cage sectors of six rollers each. Each roller weighed 546 pounds and was slightly tapered, with the outer flange being 15.19 inches in diameter and the inner flange measuring 14.25 inches. *National Archives*

The well of turret 1 is viewed on December 21, 1943. At the bottom, a ladder leads down the inside of the upper barbette to the top of the turret foundation. Below are the fixed platforms of the upper and lower projectile flats and, at the bottom, the fixed part of the powder-handling flat and, painted in a lighter color, the well of the rotating part of the powder-handling flat. Three bright-metal powder-hoist cars, which will be placed inside the powder-hoist trunks once the lower turret structure is installed, are leaning against the circular bulkhead in the powder-handling flat. *National Archives*

The lower structure of turret 3 is being lowered into the barbette on December 23, 1944. The front of the structure is facing the camera, and the upper and lower projectile flats and their circular bulkheads are in view. *National Archives*

One of the powder-hoist cars, seen in the top photo, is leaning against the circular bulkhead in the powder-handling flat of turret 1, on December 22, 1943. One of these cars will be installed in each of the three powder-hoist trunks, to carry two powder bags at a time up to the gunhouse, for loading into the 16-inch/50-caliber guns. On the left side of the car are the two operating levers for the upper and lower dumping trays. *National Archives*

CONSTRUCTION 21

By the time this photo was taken off the port bow of the *Wisconsin*, on January 17, 1944, the upper structures of all three turrets, including the 16-inch/50-caliber guns, had been installed. The gunhouses of the turrets were still under construction, with the outer shells of armor plate yet to be installed. Towering over the ship is the Philadelphia Navy Yard's 350-ton hammerhead crane. *National Archives*

As seen off the port stern of the *Wisconsin* on January 17, 1944, the armor on the side and front of the gunhouse of turret 3 remains to be installed. Although one of the twin 5-inch/38-caliber gun mounts on the port side has received its armored shield, the others still lack all or parts of their shields and are covered with canvas. *National Archives*

With the lower structure of turret 3 emplaced in the well, a unique view is provided of the upper projectile flat. Actually, the flat constitutes three concentric, ring-shaped, projectile-handling and projectile-storing platforms. The outer, dark-colored one was fixed and was for storing projectiles vertically on their bases. The center projectile-handling ring (with four wooden boxes resting on it) was a moving one, and it traversed in unison with the gunhouse and the 16-inch/50-caliber guns. Between the center platform and the circular bulkhead at the center of the flat is the rotating inner platform. This platform was for storing projectiles, and it rotated independently of the movement of the turret, in order to position projectiles close to the projectile hoists, which were yet to be installed on the center platform. Inside the circular bulkhead is machinery, including the motor for powering the inner projectile-storage ring, as well as the box-shaped trunks for the powder hoists. The left and center trunks are next to each other at the left, while the right trunk is to the right. *National Archives*

22 USS WISCONSIN (BB-64)

A sailor armed with a rifle and a bayonet stands guard on the main deck of the *Wisconsin* on May 25, 1944. To his left, and aft of turret 3, are a gallery of 20 mm antiaircraft guns and a basket containing a floating net, which in the event the ship was sunk would float free of the basket, affording survivors something to cling to until rescued. *National Archives*

CONSTRUCTION 23

CHAPTER 2
1940s Service

Wisconsin's first oceangoing voyages were brief, operating in the Delaware Bay and then Chesapeake Bay, where additional training and drills could be conducted in those protected waters, and also near the massive Navy base at Norfolk, Virginia, in the event of trouble.

During this time, the crew became finely honed, firing many rounds from each of the battleship's big guns, and practicing procedures again and again so that they could be performed almost by habit, much like breathing, in the event of emergency.

This was followed by additional training and a shakedown period in the West Atlantic and Caribbean, visiting Trinidad, the Gulf of Paria, and Puerto Rico. The ship left the Culebra range, Puerto Rico, on August 2, steaming to the Delaware Bay. It returned to the Philadelphia Navy Yard on August 10, for post-shakedown adjustments, repairs, and modifications. It left the yard on September 24 for full-speed trials the next day and on September 27, 1944, following drone firing, joined Task Group 27.3, bound for the Pacific via the Panama Canal.

It arrived in San Pedro, California, on October 12. After two days' liberty, *Wisconsin* stood out from California, bound for Pearl Harbor, in the company of *North Carolina* (BB-55), *Pasadena* (CL-65), and destroyers *Waldron*, *Haynsworth*, and *Charles. S. Sperry*.

The *Wisconsin* arrived on October 20 and was assigned to Task Force 15. It conducted additional training off Hawaii in October and spent much of November in port. Early in December, *Wisconsin*, flagship of newly formed Task Unit 12.5.9, under RAdm. Edward Hanson, commander of Battleship Division Nine, steamed toward Ulithi Atoll in the Caroline Islands.

When *Wisconsin* left Ulithi on December 11, it was assigned to Battleship Division 7, in Task Group 34, to take part in the recapture of the Philippines. But on December 18, Mother Nature put *Wisconsin* and the rest of Task Force 38 to a far-greater test than had the Japanese when the task force was engulfed by Typhoon Cobra. While three destroyers were sunk and three more were seriously damaged, as was a cruiser, and five aircraft carriers were damaged (and 146 aircraft destroyed), with 790 men lost from these vessels, *Wisconsin* survived without any significant damage other than to its aircraft, and there were no major injuries.

Wisconsin next moved to Luzon, where its powerful antiaircraft batteries protected the carriers attacking Japanese positions. The task group then moved to the South China Sea, operating against positions in Indochina, China, Hong Kong, and Okinawa.

It was off Okinawa on March 18, where *Wisconsin*'s gunners downed their first kamikaze.

On March 24, *Wisconsin* used its big guns in combat for the first time, not firing at enemy warships—the purpose for which it had been designed—but instead pounding Japanese positions on Okinawa, with the battleship firing at ranges from 17,500 to 20,000 yards.

On July 15, at the urging of Adm. Halsey, Adm. John S. McCain, commander of Task Force 38, found some big-gun work for the *Wisconsin* to do, along with *Iowa* and *Missouri*: the vicious bombardment of the steelworks at Muroran, on the northern Japanese island of Hokkaido. At ranges of 29,660 to 32,000 yards, 16-inch rounds were let loose by *Wisconsin*. This was followed on July 17–18 by a similarly blistering shelling of Hitachi on the island of Honshu, this time with the three Iowa-class ships being joined by *North Carolina* and *Alabama*.

Wisconsin arrived in Tokyo Bay on September 5, 1945, three days after the formal Japanese surrender. Briefly part of the occupying force, it soon steamed to Okinawa, where on September 22 it took aboard combat veterans as part of Operation Magic Carpet, returning troops stateside. It arrived in Pearl Harbor on October 4, remaining there for five days before steaming to San Francisco, tying up there on October 15.

In January 1946, the battleship set course for the East Coast, reaching Hampton Roads, Virginia, on January 18. Following a training cruise to Guantánamo Bay, *Wisconsin* put into the Norfolk Naval Shipyard for overhaul. After overhaul, starting in November, it took aboard midshipmen for training cruises in the Caribbean and West Atlantic. The following year was much the same, albeit including midshipmen training cruises to Europe. At the end of the year, *Wisconsin* again put into Norfolk and began the process of inactivation, becoming part of the mothball fleet. On July 1, 1948, the process complete, *Wisconsin* was decommissioned for the first time.

The *Wisconsin* is shown passing through the mouth of Delaware Bay during a shakedown cruise on May 30, 1944. Three Vought OS2U floatplanes are on the fantail: one on each catapult, and one stored on the deck. Among other duties, during shore bombardments, observers in the Kingfishers would spot the effects of the fire, radioing instructions for correcting the fire back to the battleship. *National Archives*

On June 7, 1944, a month and a half after its April 16 commissioning, USS *Wisconsin* was photographed at the Philadelphia Navy Yard. The ship was now painted in the Measure 22 camouflage it would wear through the remainder of World War II. This consisted of Navy Blue (5-N) below the lowest point of the main deck, and Haze Gray (5-H) above that line. The boot topping, the black band along the waterline of the ship, shows evidence of heavy weathering and discoloration. *National Archives*

1940s SERVICE   25

USS *Wisconsin* is cruising in the Atlantic off the Virginia Capes during a shakedown cruise, on June 8, 1944. Atop the foremast is the SK "bedspring" air-search radar antenna. On the forward fire control tower, to the front and slightly below the SK antenna, is the forward Mk. 38 main-battery director, called "Spot 1," with the rangefinder jutting from its sides and a Mk. 8 radar antenna on top. *US Navy*

An aerial photographer captured this view of the *Wisconsin* off its starboard beam in open waters near the Virginia Capes, on June 8, 1944. *US Navy*

The *Wisconsin* is viewed from the aft starboard quarter off the Virginia Capes during its shakedown period, on June 8, 1944. The decks and horizontal surfaces of the ship, under Measure 22 camouflage, were finished in Deck Blue (20-B). On the two catapults on the fantail are Vought OS2U Kingfisher observation floatplanes. *US Navy*

On June 22, 1944, USS *Wisconsin* is proceeding in the open ocean east of Virginia Beach, Virginia. The OS2U scout planes are not aboard. The dark area on the aft part of the main deck is from water that has been hosed on it, for swabbing the deck. Note the quad 40 mm gun mount on the raised platform on the roof of turret 3, to the front of which is the box-shaped splinter shield for the gun's director. *US Navy*

1940s SERVICE 27

After spending much of June 1944 in and around Chesapeake Bay, USS *Wisconsin* departed from Norfolk, Virginia, on July 7, en route to the Caribbean for further shakedown activities. This aerial photo of the port side of the ship was taken off Trinidad, British West Indies, on July 18, 1944. *US Navy*

After its shakedown cruise to the Caribbean, the *Wisconsin* returned to the Philadelphia Navy Yard for repairs and modifications to correct any problems encountered in its systems during its initial periods at sea. Here, the ship's crew, many in dress whites, line the rails while the ship is anchored off the Philadelphia Navy Yard on September 24, 1944. As built, the *Wisconsin* had an enclosed navigating bridge, whereas its sister ships *Iowa* and *New Jersey* were completed with open navigating bridges. *US Navy*

Wisconsin is viewed off its port bow at the Philadelphia Navy Yard on September 24, 1944. Of interest is the white or light-colored paint on the hull below the boot topping. The tubes of the 16-inch/50-caliber guns were painted a dark color, presumably Deck Blue, on the top halves, and a light color, evidently Haze Gray, on the lower halves. *US Navy*

1940s SERVICE 29

Three Vought OS2U Kingfishers are aboard the *Wisconsin* at Philadelphia on September 24, 1944: one on each catapult and one on the deck to the front of the starboard catapult. At the top of the mainmast is the SG surface-search radar antenna, which was quite diminutive compared with the SK "bedspring" antenna on the foremast. *US Navy*

Tugboats are coming alongside USS *Wisconsin* at the Philadelphia Navy Yard on September 24, 1944. On the fantail, rising above the catapults, is the aircraft crane, flanked by two platforms with quadruple 40 mm gun mounts. *US Navy*

The *Wisconsin* is observed from above its stern at Philadelphia on September 24, 1944. The position of the Vought OS2U Kingfisher on the deck to the front of the right catapult is apparent. Between that plane and turret 3 is a gallery of 20 mm antiaircraft guns, with protection for the battery on the sides and rear provided by a splinter shield attached to the deck. *US Navy*

The ship is viewed from the port side off a sandbar in the Delaware River at Philadelphia, on the same date as the preceding photo. Two life rafts were stored on the side of the gunhouse of each of the three turrets. *US Navy*

In an overhead view of the *Wisconsin* at Philadelphia on September 24, 1944, the graceful lines of the forward hull and bow are evident. *US Navy*

The *Wisconsin* is underway at low speed, with all three Kingfishers having departed from the battleship, in the last of the series of photos of the ship taken at Philadelphia on September 24, 1944. On this date, the ship began its voyage to the Pacific, by way of the Panama Canal, where it would join the Pacific Fleet on October 2, 1944. *US Navy*

A considerable wake follows the *Wisconsin* during a high-speed run on September 25, 1944. The ship was capable of cruising at 33 knots. The photo was taken on the day after the ship began its journey from the Atlantic coast to join the Pacific Fleet. *National Archives*

On September 26, 1944, the *Wisconsin* is riding at anchor at an unidentified harbor, with an escort in the background. The starboard boarding ladder is deployed, and toward the stern a boat boom has been rigged, to which a motor whaleboat is moored. *National Archives*

In a photo dated October 4, 1944, the *Wisconsin* is underway in Panama Bay, on the Pacific side of the Panama Canal. All three of the ship's Kingfisher floatplanes are mounted on dollies and are secured to the fantail. *National Archives*

On November 6, 1944, while in port at Pearl Harbor, USS *Wisconsin* received an official visit by Fleet Adm. Chester W. Nimitz, USN, commander in chief, Pacific–Pacific Ocean Areas (CinCPac-POA). Here, Nimitz, *third from left*, is boarding his admiral's barge at a dock at Pearl Harbor. *Naval History and Heritage Command*

Nimitz, *third from left*, salutes as he comes aboard the quarterdeck of USS *Wisconsin*. *Naval History and Heritage Command*

At Pearl Harbor on November 6, 1944, Adm. Nimitz, *left foreground*, walks on the deck of USS *Wisconsin* with its commanding officer, Capt. Earl E. Stone, *center*, and Nimitz's aide, Lt. Cdr. Hal A. Lamar, *right*. *Naval History and Heritage Command*

1940s SERVICE 35

USS *Wisconsin*, bottom, is moored alongside the hulk of the battleship *Oklahoma* (BB-37) at Pearl Harbor on November 11, 1944. The Japanese sank the *Oklahoma* during the December 7, 1941, attack; the Navy subsequently raised the ship, decommissioned it, and, as seen here, prepared it for storage until it could be towed to the West Coast for scrapping. (The *Oklahoma* sank while under tow to California on May 17, 1947.) A dreadnought battleship of another era, launched in 1914, *Oklahoma* was 304 feet shorter than the new *Wisconsin*. *Naval History and Heritage Command*

In another November 11, 1944, photo of *Wisconsin* moored at Pearl Harbor, the entrance to the harbor is in the center distance, the tank farm is in the right middle distance, and Hickam Field is in the left background. *National Archives*

A Navy photographer on the cruiser USS *Pasadena* (CL-65) took this photograph of the *Wisconsin* underway, evidently around mid-November 1944. The Mk. 37 directors, which controlled the twin 5-inch/38-caliber guns, have been refitted with combination Mk. 12 / Mk. 22 radar antennas, distinguished by the parabolic Mk. 22 antenna on the right side of the Mk. 12 antenna. The Mk. 22 antenna was nicknamed the "orange-peel antenna" because of the similarity of its shape to a segment of orange peel. *National Archives*

An original color photo depicts the band of USS *Wisconsin* performing on the main deck next to turret 3 around 1945. The bucklers, which seal the opening between the face of the turret and the 16-inch gun tubes, and the two colors of the gun tubes, Deck Blue over Haze Gray, are clearly visible. Ladders are attached to the face of the turret. *National Archives*

From a vantage point on the aft starboard part of the superstructure of USS *Wisconsin* on February 5, 1945, in the foreground is a twin 5-inch/38-caliber gun mount, beyond which are two quad 40 mm antiaircraft gun mounts. Farther ahead are the forward smokestack, the foremast, and the forward Mk. 38 primary-battery director. *National Archives*

A February 19, 1945, photo of the *Wisconsin* refueling a destroyer at sea during a raid against Japan by Task Force 58 also provides a clear view of the roof and rear of the armored shield of one of the battleship's twin 5-inch/38-caliber gun mounts. At the rear of the roof is the mount captain's hatch, the door of which is open. An equilibrator cylinder for assisting in opening and closing the door is on the rear of the shield. Around the perimeter of the roof is a toe rail. *National Archives*

A photograph dated February 1945, taken from the forward fire control tower of the *Wisconsin*, presents details of the roof of the conning tower in the foreground, the roofs and armored rangefinder hoods of turrets 1 and 2, and the forecastle. To the front of the radar antenna on the conning-tower roof is the captain's periscope, with four light-colored periscope heads also arrayed on that roof. Below the conning tower is an open bridge on the level above the pilothouse. Below that bridge is the quadruple 40 mm gun mount on the roof of turret 2, to the front of which is a box-shaped splinter guard for the Mk. 51 director for that quad 40 mm mount; the panels of the shield were hinged, and the back one is lowered. On the starboard side of the roof of turret 2 is a beam for lowering 16-inch ammunition to the magazines deep in the hull. *National Archives*

Crewmen of the quadruple 40 mm gun mount on top of turret 2 are at their stations during operations off the Japanese coast in February 1945. On the inside of the round splinter shield to the far left are stored 40 mm ammunition clips, with covers over them. To the front of the gun mount, also on the roof of turret 2, is the Mk. 51 director associated with that antiaircraft gun mount. Manned by skilled crewmen, the antiaircraft-gun directors had computing gunsights and, for backup, a ring-and-bead sight, on a pedestal mount, for the purpose of acquiring and tracking enemy aircraft. Through the director, the operator was able to aim and fire the associated guns. *National Archives*

The three types of antiaircraft artillery employed on USS *Wisconsin* in World War II are viewed from above, from the starboard side of the forward fire-control tower. In the bottom foreground and also farther down toward the left are two quadruple 40 mm gun mounts on circular platforms. In the small tub below the whip antenna is the Mk. 51 director for the lower quad 40 mm gun mount. To the lower right is a twin 5-inch/38-caliber gun mount; note the toe rail around the roof of the gun shield. Below that gun mount are two 20 mm guns, with ammunition lockers for them to their rears. *National Archives*

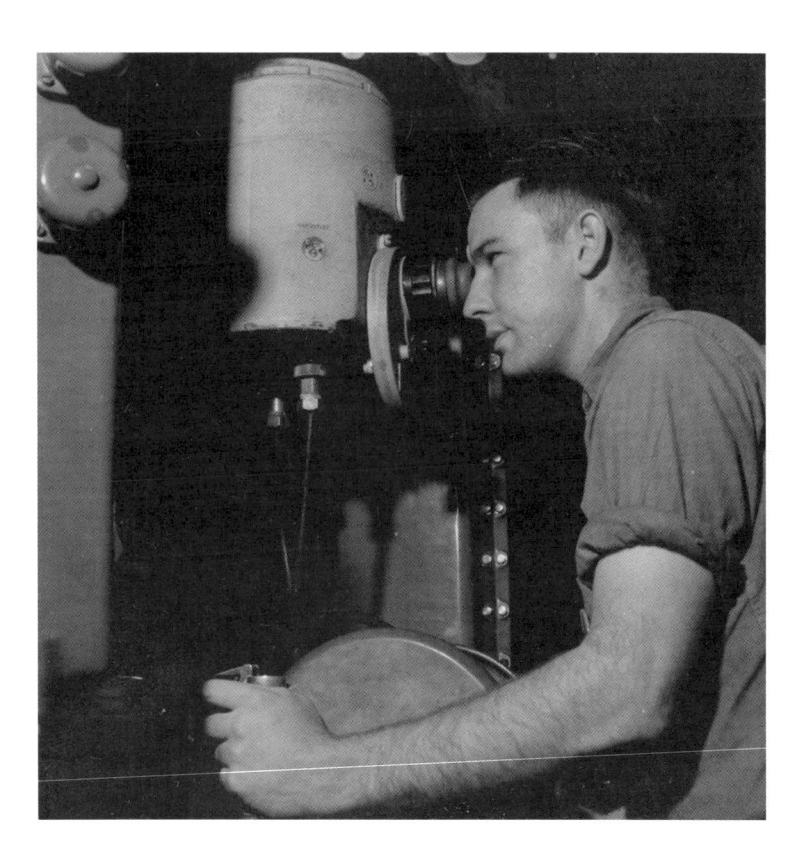

Fire Controlman 3rd Class G. R. Pierre peers through a periscope as he operates the fire-control trainer in main-battery control, located in the top level of the conning tower of USS *Wisconsin*. *National Archives*

A crewman is on a ladder in one of the projectile flats, in the depths of a 16-inch/50-caliber gun turret on USS *Wisconsin* sometime before late May 1945. To the right are 16-inch projectiles on the inner ring of the flat, while to the left and center are more projectiles on the fixed part of the flat. The projectiles in the flats were stored upright, on their bases, secured with chains. *National Archives*

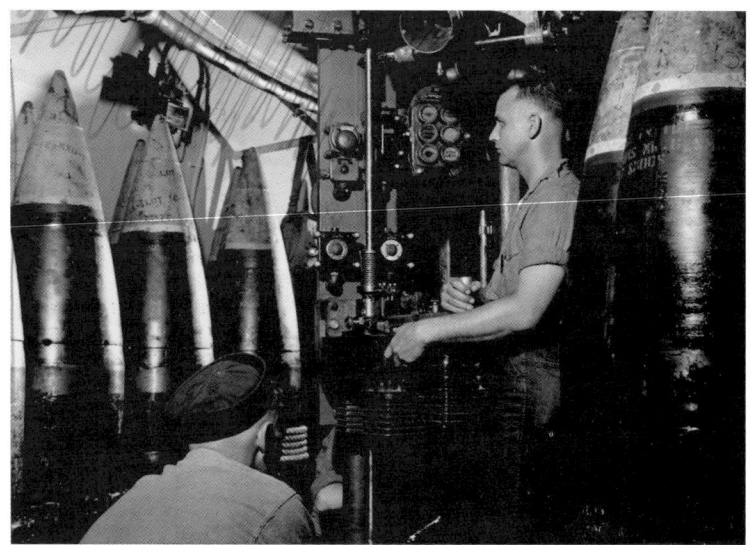

Each projectile flat, of which there were two per turret, had three projectile hoists, located on the center ring of the flat. Each projectile hoist had one operator, one of whom is shown here at his station. He operated the hoist going by visual and audible signals and warnings of dial indicators (the panel of six round indicators to the front of the operator's head) and a gong. The ribbed objects below the operator's left arm are solenoids. *National Archives*

A projectile is visible deep inside a projectile hoist on USS *Wisconsin*, making its way up to a turret for loading into a 16-inch gun. *National Archives*

Lt. (junior grade) Phillip S. Bowman, an assistant turret officer, is looking through the port periscope in the turret officer's booth in one of the 16-inch gun turrets on USS *Wisconsin* in 1945. The turret officer's booth was the compartment that took up the entire width of the gunhouse of each turret, to the rear of the gun-room compartments. It housed the rammer motors and mechanisms, a rangefinder, two periscopes, an auxiliary fire-control computer, the turret officer's transfer switchboard, and other equipment. *National Archives*

In the center rear of the turret officer's booth of one of the *Wisconsin*'s turrets, the crew of the rangefinder is at work. *From left to right*, they are the pointer, who controlled the rangefinder's elevation and depression; the rangefinder operator; and the trainer, who controlled the instrument's azimuth. The operator remained on standby during action, except when the turret was being used as a gun director or when the turret was under local control, in which case he transmitted range data verbally to the computer operator. *National Archives*

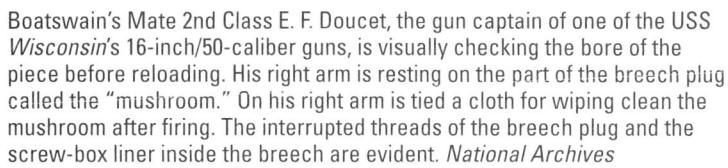

Boatswain's Mate 2nd Class E. F. Doucet, the gun captain of one of the USS *Wisconsin*'s 16-inch/50-caliber guns, is visually checking the bore of the piece before reloading. His right arm is resting on the part of the breech plug called the "mushroom." On his right arm is tied a cloth for wiping clean the mushroom after firing. The interrupted threads of the breech plug and the screw-box liner inside the breech are evident. *National Archives*

Gun captain Doucet is supervising the ramming of a 16-inch projectile into one of the big guns of USS *Wisconsin* sometime before late May 1945. Loading the projectiles and powder charges into the 16-inch/50-caliber guns was an intricate, highly rehearsed procedure, with little room for error. Stamped on the rear face of the breech is data on the gun, including the information that it was a 16-inch gun Mk. 7 Mod 0, serial number 308, made by the US Naval Gun Factory, Washington Navy Yard. *National Archives*

On the powder flat at the bottom of one of the *Wisconsin*'s turrets, a powder handler is lifting a powder charge weighing 110 pounds up to a car in one of the powder hoists. It took six of these powder bags to fire a 16-inch projectile. *National Archives*

Once the 16-inch projectile was rammed into the gun, the six bagged powder charges were sent up to the top of a powder hoist, arriving to the rear of the breech. The door of the hoist was opened, and, as seen here, the charges were rolled out and onto a spanning tray, ready for ramming into the gun. *National Archives*

Gun captain Doucet and another crewman are lining up powder charges for ramming into a 16-inch gun on USS *Wisconsin*. *National Archives*

On March 15, 1945, one day after departing from Ulithi with Task Force 58 bound for Okinawa, crew members of the *Wisconsin* are preparing small, radio-controlled target drones for launching from the port catapult. Two drones are under assembly in the foreground, and another one is on the catapult, ready for launching. *National Archives*

A 4.5-pound "no-load" charge has just been fired to launch a radio-controlled target drone from the port catapult of USS *Wisconsin* on or around March 15, 1945. Note the life rafts stored on the deck, below the catapult. *National Archives*

Four radio-controlled target drones are being readied on the fantail of the *Wisconsin* on March 15, 1945. The small planes would give the crews of the ship's antiaircraft batteries an opportunity to sharpen their skills before facing the real thing off Okinawa. In the background is one of the ship's Vought OS2U Kingfishers. *National Archives*

The assembly process for the radio-controlled target drones is viewed from another perspective on the fantail of USS *Wisconsin* on March 15, 1945. *National Archives*

A Kingfisher has just been launched from the starboard catapult of USS *Wisconsin* on March 27, 1945, and is visible over the water to the front of the catapult. To the upper right are the platform and safety rails for the SG surface-search radar. *National Archives*

Partially obscured by the rigging lines to the left of center, a Kingfisher has landed off the port beam of USS *Wisconsin* on March 27, 1945, and soon will be brought back aboard with the aircraft crane. The *Wisconsin*'s catapult-launched spotter planes were assigned to Observation Squadron 10 (VO-10). *National Archives*

A Kingfisher scout plane is being lowered onto the port catapult of the battleship *Wisconsin* after a mission on March 27, 1945. The plane is numbered "1" on the cowling, and an insignia of what appears to be Disney art is on the tail; it depicted a cartoon duck holding a telescope. *National Archives*

A fuller view of the cartoon duck insignia on the tail is available in this photo of Kingfisher number 2 on the starboard catapult of USS *Wisconsin* on March 27, 1945. Assignments of floatplanes to battleships by model and numbers varied from month to month during World War II. For example, in December 1944, two Kingfishers were on the *Wisconsin*: a Vought OS2U-3 and an OS2N-1, a version of the plane manufactured by the Naval Aircraft Factory, Philadelphia, Pennsylvania. *National Archives*

1940s SERVICE 45

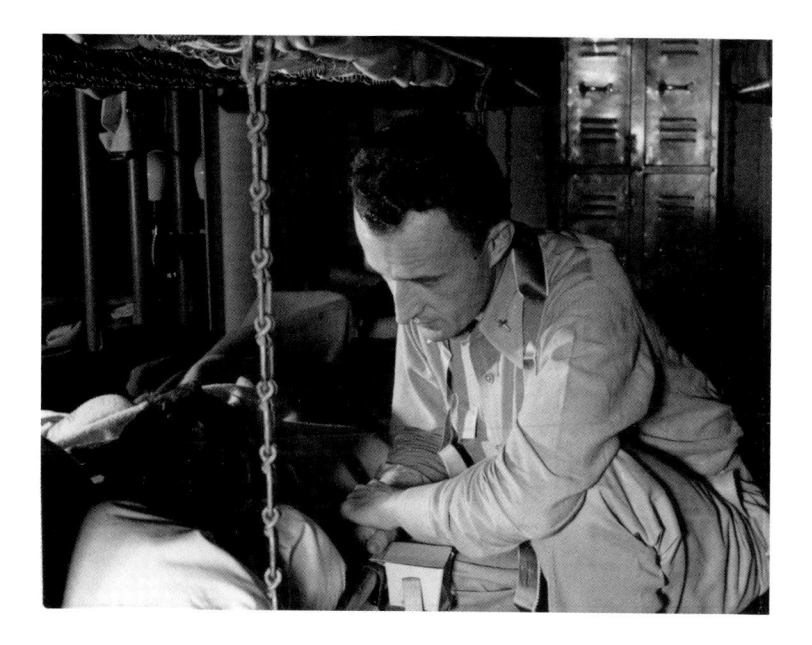

Chaplain Gordian V. Ehrlacher, a Catholic priest and formerly a missionary in China, ministers to Seaman 1st Class William A. Berryman, who was wounded in action on another ship and transferred to *Wisconsin* for treatment. The photo was taken on June 18, 1945, at which time the ship was anchored in Leyte Gulf, in the Philippines, undergoing repairs and resupply. *National Archives*

On July 15, 1945, USS *Wisconsin* is bombarding industrial plants in the vicinity of Muroran, along the coast of Hokkaido, Japan. The ship was operating with Task Unit 34.8.2, which included two of *Wisconsin*'s sister ships, USS *Iowa* (BB-61) and USS *Missouri* (BB-63), one of which is visible in the right background. By this stage of the war, US battleships were able to shell Japanese cities along the coastline with virtual impunity. *National Archives*

The *Wisconsin* is viewed from a different perspective as its 16-inch guns unleash a salvo against an industrial plant near Muroran, Hokkaido, on July 15, 1945. This photo and the preceding one were taken from USS *Dayton* (CL-105). *National Archives*

As seen from an unidentified destroyer, USS *Wisconsin*, *left background*, and another destroyer, *right*, are being refueled by the fleet oiler USS *Lackawanna* (AO-40) during August 1945. A redesigned mainmast is apparent, which also is visible in the July 15, 1945, photographs. The top of the mast had been extended, with a new platform toward its top, and with the SG surface-search antenna at the top of the mast. *National Archives*

USS *Wisconsin*'s air group provided rescue support for the final USN air strike on Tokyo, on August 13, 1945. The ship as seen here was photographed from the Essex-class carrier USS *Shangri-La* (CV-38) four days later, on August 17, just two days after Emperor Hirohito's declaration of the surrender of the Japanese Empire. *National Archives*

A Navy photographer aboard USS *Wasp* (CV-18) snapped this photo of the *Wisconsin* passing the carrier in the West Pacific, on August 22, 1945. The ship still wore the Measure 22 camouflage paint it entered service in. *National Archives*

On October 4, 1945, USS *Wisconsin* arrived at Pearl Harbor, transporting GIs from Okinawa back to the United States in an operation called Magic Carpet. The *Wisconsin* is seen here during that visit to Pearl, moored on the opposite side of USS *Arkansas*, a dreadnought battleship launched in 1911 and still in commission at that time. The *Wisconsin* so exceeded the *Arkansas* in length that much of the former's stern is visible to the left, and the hull from turret 1 forward is in view to the right. At a time when the US Navy's battleships were being supplied increasingly with the new Curtiss SC Seahawk floatplanes, a Kingfisher is on the *Wisconsin*'s starboard catapult. *National Archives*

USS *Wisconsin* arrived at San Francisco, California, on October 15, 1945, with a consignment of returning servicemen, under Operation Magic Carpet. The ship is seen here anchored off San Francisco on October 23, 1945. What appears to be a movie screen is rigged to the aircraft crane on the fantail. Landing craft and motorboats, some with sailors aboard departing for or returning from shore leave, are near the ship. *National Archives*

48 USS WISCONSIN (BB-64)

During a cruise from the Panama Canal to Valparaiso, Chile, in late October 1946, the *Wisconsin* crossed the equator. Hence, a Neptune Party, also called "crossing the line," was called for. In this ancient ritual, sailors who have never before crossed the equator, called "pollywogs," are hazed by members of Neptune's court, after which they are initiated as "trusty shellbacks." Here, pollywogs of USS *Wisconsin* are bowing as Neptune strides past them. *National Archives*

In late 1946, the *Wisconsin* visited several South American ports. It is seen here dressed fore and aft with pennants in honor of an inspection tour by President Gabriel González Videla, of Chile, at Valparaiso on November 5, 1946. Three Curtiss SC-1 Seahawks are on the catapults. By this time, the SK bedspring surface-search antenna on the foretop had been replaced by a round SK-2 surface-search radar antenna. *National Archives*

1940s SERVICE 49

In early January 1947, USS *Wisconsin* departed from the Norfolk Naval Base, in Virginia, on a twelve-day training cruise to the Caribbean with 565 US Naval Reserve officers and enlisted men. Two Navy tugboats are assisting it to the dock upon its return to Norfolk on January 18. Note the dark-colored covers over the barrels of the quad 40 mm guns. The bow exhibits slightly different shades of Haze Gray paint from touch-ups, and there are several dark shapes, evidently primer or areas where the Haze Gray paint eroded. *Norfolk Public Library*

In a photo taken within moments of the preceding image, a girl with a dog watches from a dock as tugboats maneuver USS *Wisconsin* at Norfolk Naval Shipyard on January 18, 1947. *Norfolk Public Library*

USS *Wisconsin* is viewed off its starboard bow as it approaches its berth at Norfolk on January 18, 1947. The dark areas on the forward hull are apparently from priming. *Norfolk Public Library*

In another view of *Wisconsin* approaching the dock at Norfolk, note the venturi windscreen on the front of the splinter shield for the 20 mm guns on the forecastle. This feature was on the ship as built. It served to direct the airstream upward when the ship was in motion, to spare the crewmen at the 20 mm guns from the wind. *Norfolk Public Library*

1940s SERVICE 51

Civilians and sailors await the docking of the *Wisconsin* at Norfolk on January 18, 1947. On the side of the top of the hull, *to the far right*, is a stored boat boom, which was swung out when the ship was anchored in a harbor, to allow boats to moor to it. *Norfolk Public Library*

A view of the *Wisconsin* approaching a dock at the Norfolk Naval Base provides clear details of the forward part of the superstructure, including the enclosed navigating bridge, the front of the conning tower, and the forward fire-control tower. The conning tower was a structure at the front of the superstructure with armor 17.5 inches thick, which housed navigating and fire-control stations for use during battle. *Norfolk Public Library*

Sailors are hauling on a hawser, preparing to moor USS *Wisconsin* to a dock at the Norfolk Naval Base on January 18, 1947. The tripod apparatus on the main deck toward the left is a mast for handling a paravane, which is a towed, submersible device for cutting the mooring cables of submerged mines. *Norfolk Public Library*

Officers, sailors, and civilians have congregated on the main deck of the *Wisconsin* while the ship is being docked at Norfolk. During the twelve-day training cruise to the Caribbean in January 1947, a dozen members of the press were aboard. In the right background is the cruiser USS *Providence* (CL-82). *Norfolk Public Library*

Crewmen are using the gangplanks abeam the rear of turret 3 (*left*) during the *Wisconsin*'s return to Norfolk in January 1947. Note the ship's bell below the platform under the aft Mk. 37 secondary-battery director to the left of center. More toward the right is the aft fire-control tower, with the aft Mk. 38 primary-battery director on top of it. *Norfolk Public Library*

Upon the return of the USS *Wisconsin* to the Norfolk Naval Base on January 18, 1947, two of the members of the press who were guests on the twelve-day training voyage to the Caribbean, *Norfolk Ledger-Dispatch* editor Lenoir Chambers and radio announcer E. N. "Jim" McWilliams, confer on the main deck. *Norfolk Public Library*

On February 10, 1947, the *Wisconsin* is departing from Cristobal, on the Caribbean side of the Canal Zone, during another two-week US Naval Reserve training cruise. Typically, the crew of the battleship was allowed two days' liberty during the visit to the Canal Zone. *National Archives*

A photographer aboard the aircraft carrier USS *Randolph* (CV-15) snapped this photo of the *Wisconsin* during a cruise on August 1, 1947. Three Curtiss Seahawks are visible: two are on the catapults, and one is on the fantail. *National Archives*

During a cruise to the Panama Canal from October 13 to 24, 1947, USS *Wisconsin* is riding at anchor at an unidentified harbor. Boarding ladders are deployed along the hull abeam turret 1 and the rear of the superstructure. On the main deck between turret 3 and the catapults is a postwar addition: a projection booth for showing movies on the fantail. *Richard A. Pestke via USS* Wisconsin *Association*

Water splashes over the foredeck of the *Wisconsin* while underway in October 1947. In the center foreground, on the roof of turret 2, is the box-shaped splinter shield for the director for the quadruple 40 mm antiaircraft gun mount on the rear of the same roof. *Richard A. Pestke via USS* Wisconsin *Association*

On the foredeck, several members of the crew of the *Wisconsin* are painting some links of the port anchor chain during a cruise in October 1947. Next to them is an open hatch. Farther aft is the port wildcat, which operates the port anchor chain. To the rear of the wildcat, two sailors are standing at the horizontal control wheels of the wildcat. *Richard A. Pestke via USS* Wisconsin *Association*

Sailors dressed in whites are assembled on the fantail of USS *Wisconsin* during the October 1947 cruise to the Panama Canal. To the right are two twin 20 mm gun mounts with the guns not installed. Just aft of these gun mounts are a ventilator and a winch. To the left is the right hood for the rangefinder of turret 3. *Richard A. Pestke via USS* Wisconsin *Association*

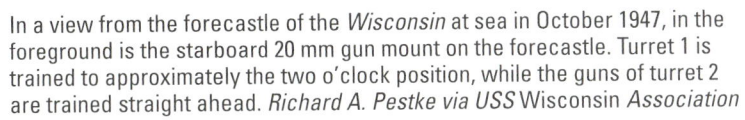

In a view from the forecastle of the *Wisconsin* at sea in October 1947, in the foreground is the starboard 20 mm gun mount on the forecastle. Turret 1 is trained to approximately the two o'clock position, while the guns of turret 2 are trained straight ahead. *Richard A. Pestke via USS* Wisconsin *Association*

In a photo taken from the forecastle of the *Wisconsin*, probably within moments of the preceding photo, crewmen in the foreground are working on the starboard anchor chain while one of the twin 5-inch/38-caliber gun mounts is firing in the background. *Richard A. Pestke via USS* Wisconsin *Association*

Turrets 1 and 2 and the foredeck of the *Wisconsin* are viewed from above during a 1947 cruise. Beams for lowering 16-inch projectiles to the magazines in the depths of the hull are mounted on the turret roofs: there are two on the port side of turret 1, and one on the starboard side of turret 2. Toward the top of the photo are splinter shields for 40 mm and 20 mm antiaircraft guns. *Richard A. Pestke via USS* Wisconsin *Association*

1940s SERVICE 57

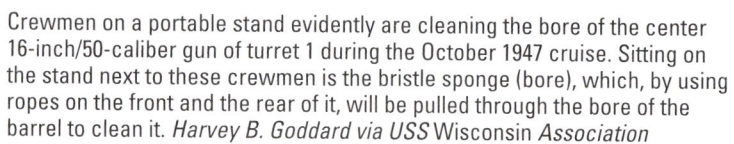

Crewmen on a portable stand evidently are cleaning the bore of the center 16-inch/50-caliber gun of turret 1 during the October 1947 cruise. Sitting on the stand next to these crewmen is the bristle sponge (bore), which, by using ropes on the front and the rear of it, will be pulled through the bore of the barrel to clean it. *Harvey B. Goddard via USS* Wisconsin *Association*

A gunner is operating a twin 20 mm antiaircraft gun mount on the *Wisconsin* in October 1947. Only the left gun has the ammunition magazine attached. The gunner is using a Mk. 14 gyro gunsight. The gun shield, carriage, and pedestal exhibit what appears to be zinc chromate primer. *Harvey B. Goddard via USS* Wisconsin *Association*

In January 1948, USS *Wisconsin* joined the Atlantic Reserve Fleet at Norfolk, Virginia, and the months-long process of preparing it for inactivation and long-term storage began. In March 1948, the battleship entered drydock, and on the twenty-ninth of the month this photo of one of the two rudders was taken, with the front of the rudder to the right. *Norfolk Navy Yard*

USS *Wisconsin* Data

Builder	Philadelphia Navy Yard
Laid down	January 25, 1941
Launched	December 7, 1943
Commissioned	April 16, 1944
Decommissioned	July 1, 1948
Recommissioned	March 3, 1951
Decommissioned	March 8, 1958
Recommissioned	October 22, 1988
Decommissioned	September 30, 1991
Struck	January 12, 1995
Reinstated	February 12, 1998
Struck	March 17, 2006
Class	Iowa
Sponsor	Madge (Mrs. Walter) Goodland
Displacement, standard	45,000 tons
Displacement, full load, 1945	57,216 tons
Displacement, full load, 1988	57,500 tons
Length, waterline, full load	860 feet
Length, overall	887 feet, 3 inches
Beam, waterline, full load	108 feet, 2 inches
Beam, maximum	108 feet, 2 inches
Design draft	34 feet, 9¼ inches
Bunker fuel	8,624 tons (1945)
Endurance (design)	14,890 nautical miles @ 15 knots
Boilers	eight Babcock & Wilcox, 565 psi
Machinery	four Westinghouse geared turbines, 212,000 total shaft horsepower
Speed	33 knots
Armor	12.2-inch belt; 5 inches on 50 lbs., armor deck; 60 lbs. on bomb deck; 11.2-inch bulkheads; 17.3-inch conning tower; 17.3-inch barbettes; 17-inch gunhouses
Armament, December 1944	Nine 16 inch / 50 cal. in three triple turrets, twenty dual 5 inch / 38 cal. gun mounts; twenty quad 40 mm mounts, forty-nine 20 mm single mounts, two 20 mm twin mounts
Armament, April 1945	Nine 16 inch / 50 cal. in three triple turrets, twenty dual 5 inch / 38 cal. gun mounts; twenty quad 40 mm mounts, forty-nine 20 mm single mounts, eight 20 mm twin mounts.
Armament, July 1988	Nine 16 inch / 50 cal. in three triple turrets, twelve dual 5 inch / 38 cal. gun mounts; thirty-two BGM-109 Tomahawk, sixteen RGM-84 Harpoon, four 20 mm CIWS
Crew, 1945:	173 officers, 2,738 enlisted
Crew, 1988:	65 officers, 1,445 enlisted

During preparations for placing the *Wisconsin* in long-term storage, one of its propellers, which had a crack in it, was removed and is seen here secured to a railroad flatcar on March 30, 1948. Although the stand is obscuring a good part of the propeller blades, this appears to be a five-bladed inboard propeller, 18.25 feet in diameter. The two outboard propellers had four blades and were 17 feet in diameter. *Norfolk Navy Yard*

The decommissioned battleship *Wisconsin*, right, is in long-term storage with the Norfolk Group, US Atlantic Reserve Fleet, in August 1948. To the left is the carrier USS *Midway*. *Mike Rigdon via USS* Wisconsin *Association*

In an aerial photo taken in August 1948, the *Wisconsin* is moored to a dock at Norfolk. Three temporary shelters are on the main deck aft of turret 3. *Mike Rigdon via USS Wisconsin Association*

The battleship *Wisconsin* is observed from the front while stored at Norfolk, Virginia, in August 1948. *Mike Rigdon via USS Wisconsin Association*

CHAPTER 3
1950s Service

Wisconsin's retirement was short lived; following the North Korean invasion of South Korea in June 1950, it, along with the rest of the Iowa-class battleships, was reactivated. All the preservation measures carefully put in place in 1948 were removed, and on March 3, 1951, the ship was recommissioned. While the ship resembled its World War II appearance, noticeably absent were the 20 mm antiaircraft guns and the aircraft catapults, the latter no longer needed with the helicopters now embarked. With many of its crew being recalled reservists, the battleship once again steamed for Europe on two midshipmen training cruises, before finally leaving for the Pacific on October 25, 1951. It reached Japan on November 21 and relieved *New Jersey* as flagship of the Seventh Fleet, with VAdm. Harold Martin commanding.

After initially escorting aircraft carriers, on December 2 *Wisconsin* took its place on the gun line, firing at the enemy in the Kasong-Kosong area. In what was arguably one of the most overkill combat situations ever, *Wisconsin*'s number 2 turret fired on an enemy T-34 tank, the results being compared by one observer to "potting a mouse with an elephant gun. There isn't much left of the mouse."

Wisconsin continued to provide gunfire support until just before Christmas, when it rejoined the carrier task force.

On January 9, the day after the ship returned to Korean waters following a brief spell in Japan, South Korean president Syngman Rhee and his wife came aboard. The year 1952 was much like the end of 1951, with *Wisconsin* delivering heavy firepower on call to support troops ashore.

On March 15, 1952, the enemy successfully struck back at *Wisconsin* for the only time in its career. A North Korean shore battery of four 152 mm guns had the misfortune of firing on the big battleship, and one of the four rounds found its mark. The result was slight damage to a 40 mm gun shield, and three men wounded. This did not set well with *Wisconsin* captain Henry Bruton and the crew, who responded with a salvo from the mighty 16-inch rifles, obliterating the enemy gun position. An escorting ship flashed the signal "Temper, temper" to *Wisconsin* as the smoke cleared from the 16-inch muzzles.

Relieved by *Iowa* on April 1, *Wisconsin* began steaming for home, stopping briefly in Guam to aid in a test of a new floating drydock. It arrived in Long Beach on April 19, then steamed on to its home port of Norfolk.

Things were routine there for *Wisconsin*, consisting of training cruises and an overhaul. During this time, a nuclear warhead for the 16-inch naval gun was developed. The Mk. 23 round was a 15–20-kiloton-yield weapon derived from the Army's 280 mm atomic cannon round. Modifications were made to enable the *Wisconsin* to store and assemble these rounds. The standard allowance was ten of the nuclear rounds and nine Mk. 24 practice rounds, and a single drill projectile. Provisions for these rounds were made in the turret 2 magazine.

Following overhaul, *Wisconsin* resumed its routine of training cruises and NATO exercises until May 6, 1956, when things became decidedly not routine. On that Sunday afternoon, *Wisconsin* was operating with the carrier *Coral Sea* (CVA-43) and escorts in a heavy fog off the Virginia coast. At 1514, the signal was heard from *Coral Sea* that a man had been lost overboard, and a destroyer set out to recover him. USS *Eaton*, DDE-510, a Fletcher-class destroyer modified for antisubmarine warfare, crossed *Wisconsin*'s bow at distance of about 200 yards. *Wisconsin* ordered back emergency full in an effort to minimize damage. However, about six seconds after the battleship sighted the *Eaton*, the towering bow of the *Wisconsin* began to slice through the forecastle of the destroyer between mounts 1 and 2, pushing the number 1 mount over the side.

Somewhat ironically, no sailor had actually gone overboard from the *Coral Sea*; rather, one had lost his hat, which a lookout had mistaken for a man. *Eaton*'s course had been ordered not by its captain, Cmdr. Richard Varley, but by Escort Destroyer Division 22 commander Capt. Terrell H. W. Connor, who happened to be on *Eaton*'s bridge at the time.

While the massive battleship had very nearly cut the 2,900-ton *Eaton* in two, the *Wisconsin* itself had by no means escaped damage. Flooding aboard the battleship was forward of frame 12, its main deck was buckled at frame 8, and there was serious damage to the bow.

With *Wisconsin* scheduled to conduct summer midshipmen cruises to Europe, there was considerable urgency to complete the repairs. To do so, the Navy towed the 72 percent complete sister ship *Kentucky* to shipway 10 of Newport News Shipbuilding and Dry Dock Company, where a 68-foot, 140-ton section of the ship's bow was cut free and loaded on a crane barge. The barge was then moved to Norfolk Navy Yard, where a similarly sized portion of *Wisconsin*'s bow had been cut up. The upper portions of the bows were of different designs, so second cuts were made in both, so that the undamaged upper portion of the *Wisconsin*'s bow could be reinstalled. The unused upper portion of *Kentucky*'s bow was stored on the upper deck of the *Kentucky*.

Sixteen days later, on June 8, the repaired *Wisconsin* left the drydock. Despite the extreme measures to repair *Wisconsin*, the following year it was slated for retirement and to return to the mothball fleet.

Its last cruise of the decade ended on November 6, 1957, when it docked in New York City after a brief voyage from Norfolk. Two days later it entered the New York Navy Yard annex in Bayonne, New Jersey, to begin inactivation overhaul. It was placed out of commission in Bayonne on March 8, 1958, leaving the US Navy without an active battleship for the first time since 1895.

The *Wisconsin* is waterborne in drydock at the Norfolk Navy Shipyard in or around January 1951. It was being brought out of long-term storage for service in the Korean War. By March 3 of that year, when the battleship was recommissioned, it would be fully refurbished, rerigged, and ready for active operations. *Norfolk Public Library*

Sailors and dock workers are managing hawsers during the drydocking of the *Wisconsin* on the same date as the preceding photograph. The small objects casting shadows on the side of the forward hull are eyes, from which riggings for staging planks were attached when sailors or workers needed access to the hull, either afloat or in drydock. *Norfolk Public Library*

On March 3, 1951, the crew and officers of USS *Wisconsin* are gathered on the main deck for the recommissioning ceremony, in which the ship was returned to active status. In the foreground are the rears of the Mk. 12 (*left*) and Mk. 22 (*right*) antennas on top of the aft Mk. 37 secondary-battery director. The catapults had been removed from the fantail. *Norfolk Public Library*

In July 1948, the *Wisconsin* was decommissioned and placed in long-term storage at the Norfolk Naval Shipyard, Portsmouth, Virginia. With the outbreak of war in Korea and a new need for battleships to bombard enemy shore installations and control the seas around the Korean Peninsula, the *Wisconsin* was brought out of mothballs. The ship is seen here with a dome-shaped "igloo," for keeping the elements out of a quadruple 40 mm gun, mount being removed by crane on January 8, 1951. The bucklers had been removed from turret 1. *Norfolk Public Library*

USS *Wisconsin* is at sea on July 10, 1951. Following the battleship's recommissioning shakedown training, it completed two US Naval Academy midshipmen training cruises during the summer of 1951, with visits to New York City; Halifax, Nova Scotia; Edinburgh, Scotland; Lisbon, Portugal; and Guantánamo Bay, Cuba. At least two motorboats are stored on the fantail, to the front of the aircraft crane. *US Navy*

During a visit to New York on the morning of August 22, 1951, USS *Wisconsin* went aground in the Hudson River adjacent to 79th Street, Manhattan. Here, seven tugboats are pushing against the starboard side of the hull, in an effort to free the battleship. *US Navy*

In a view off the stern of the *Wisconsin,* tugboats work to free the battleship while it was grounded on the Hudson River on August 22, 1951. At least eight ship's boats are stored on the main deck alongside and aft of turret 3. The rectangular object to the front of the aircraft crane probably was a movie screen. *US Navy*

The 16-inch/50-caliber guns of turret 1 are being fired at enemy positions along the Korean coast. The *Wisconsin* arrived off Korea with Task Force 77 in late November 1951. On December 2, it conducted its first Korean War bombardment of enemy forces, in the vicinity of Kasong. *National Museum of the US Navy*

The right 16-inch/50-caliber gun of turret 1 has just been fired, off the coast of Korea. The center and left guns have been lowered for reloading. *National Archives*

A Navy photographer in the foreground, on the starboard side of the forward end of the 01 level, is snapping a photo as President Rhee visits USS *Wisconsin* in port in January 1952. To the left is turret 2, with a particularly clear view of the right armored hood of the rangefinder. On the turret roof are life rafts; on the rear of the turret is a bin for floater nets: large nets with floats attached, which would provide the ship's crew with a means of staying afloat if the ship were sunk. *H. L. Green via USS* Wisconsin *Association*

The guns of turret 1 have just unleashed a volley of 16-inch shells off the Korean coastline on January 30, 1952. The guns of turret 2 are poised, ready for firing. To the lower left are a dish-type radar antenna and the top of the coning tower. *National Museum of the US Navy*

The *Wisconsin* cruises in waters between Japan and the Korean Peninsula sometime between January and April 1952. The decks are unpainted teak. The black bucklers, also called blast bags, on the turret fronts contrast with the Haze Gray paint on the turrets. *National Archives*

1950s SERVICE 67

A crewman on the USS *Wisconsin* pauses for a moment of prayer next to a poster urging sailors to worship regularly. Attached with a paper clip to the poster is a card with a schedule for Catholic masses and Protestant and Jewish services. *National Archives*

Enlisted crewmen standing in the chow line and their servers pause to say grace while USS *Wisconsin* is operating in Korean waters in March 1952. *National Archives*

The 16-inch/50-caliber main-battery guns of USS *Wisconsin*'s turrets 1 and 2 are firing at Communist rail-transportation lines along the east coast of North Korea in March 1952. Note the rivets on the turret roofs, the two periscope heads on the roof of turret 1, and the splinter shield for the 40 mm gun director on the roof of turret 2, in the foreground. *National Archives*

The three 16-inch/50-caliber guns of turret 3 of the *Wisconsin* have just fired at a railway tunnel in the Chaho-Songjin area of the eastern coast of North Korea, around mid-March 1952. In the foreground, twin 5-inch/38-caliber and 40 mm guns are trained to starboard. *National Archives*

During World War II, when a US Navy ship in the theater of war in the Pacific required below-the-waterline repairs or maintenance, it was necessary for the ship to proceed to a drydock at Pearl Harbor or on the West Coast of the United States. When a damaged ship had to leave the theater for repairs, it left the Navy at a disadvantage and could mean the difference between victory and defeat in battle. On April 4 and 5, 1952, USS *Wisconsin* made a successful, experimental docking in USS AFDB-1, the Navy's largest auxiliary floating drydock, at Apra Harbor, Guam. This experiment is documented in the following series of photos. Here, the battleship is beginning to enter the sunken drydock. *US Navy*

The *Wisconsin* is entering USS AFDB-1 within a moment of the preceding photo. At this point in time, the quadruple 40 mm gun mounts were still on the ship, for antiaircraft defense. Two of those mounts are visible to the front of turret 1. The 20 mm guns had been removed from the ship over five years earlier. *US Navy*

The ship is viewed from off the port bow while entering the floating drydock. The ship is wearing its postwar camouflage of Haze Gray on vertical surfaces above the boot topping, Deck Gray on horizontal surfaces, and Black on the upper parts of the smokestacks and mainmast. *Naval History and Heritage Command*

The forward half of the *Wisconsin* has moved into the floating drydock. In the foreground is a large crane, mounted on tracks on the top deck, referred to as the wing deck, so that it could roll to wherever needed. A similar crane was on the opposite side of the floating drydock. *Naval History and Heritage Command*

The ship is seen from the starboard side at about the same instant the preceding photo was taken. Atop the forward Mk. 38 main-battery director at the top of the forward fire-control tower is a Mk. 13 radar antenna, which has a teardrop-shaped side profile. Clear views are available of the foremast, mounted on the rear of the forward fire-control tower, and the mainmast, on the rear of the aft smokestack. *Naval History and Heritage Command*

An overhead view of the *Wisconsin* entering the floating drydock provides details of the foretop, the forward Mk. 38 primary-battery director and its Mk. 13 radar, the port side of the forward fire-control tower, and the forward part of the superstructure. During this period, the ship's antiaircraft firepower consisted of its twin 5-inch/38-caliber guns and its quadruple 40 mm guns, many of which are seen here. *Naval History and Heritage Command*

Tugboats are pushing USS *Wisconsin* into AFDB-1 at Apra Harbor, Guam, on April 5, 1952. The cover of the Mk. 13 radar antenna housing on the aft Mk. 38 director has been removed, exposing the frame underneath. Two boats are stored on the deck next to the guns of turret 3. The small deckhouse aft of the center gun of turret 3 was a movie projection booth. *Naval History and Heritage Command*

The *Wisconsin* is ensconced in the floating drydock. On the near end of the dock are the two wings of the hinged communication bridge, which would be swung together when a ship was in the dock. In the background is the communication bridge on the other end of the floating drydock. To the right are USS *APL-5*, a non-self-propelled barracks ship, and a smaller, unidentified ship alongside it. *Naval History and Heritage Command*

The communication bridge on AFDB-1 astern of USS *Wisconsin* has been closed, allowing personnel to cross over from one wing deck to the other. *Naval History and Heritage Command*

The fantail of the *Wisconsin* is viewed from above in the floating drydock, showing the communication bridge. On each side of the aircraft crane is a quad 40 mm gun mount in a circular splinter shield. To the front of each gun mount is a smaller circular splinter shield, enclosing the director for the gun mount. *Naval History and Heritage Command*

Many details of the forward superstructure and turrets 1 and 2 of USS *Wisconsin* are visible in this view of the ship while in floating drydock at Guam. To the upper left are the forward surface-search and air-search radar antennas on the foretop. To the front of the foretop is the forward Mk. 38 main-battery director, with the housings for the rangefinder jutting from its sides, and a Mk. 13 radar on top. To the starboard of the forward twin 5-inch/38-caliber gun mount is a platform that originally held two 20 mm antiaircraft guns; it now held a saluting gun. *Naval History and Heritage Command*

Once the *Wisconsin* was correctly positioned in the floating drydock, air was pumped into the pontoons on the bottom of the dock structure, expelling the water in them and giving the drydock buoyancy. In this photo, the floating drydock has risen about 8 feet, exposing the upper part of the *Wisconsin*'s hull below the waterline. *Naval History and Heritage Command*

The forward part of the *Wisconsin* is displayed in a photo taken above the floating drydock. Below the three 16-inch/50-caliber guns to the right is the breakwater. Farther forward are the two forward quadruple 40 mm gun mounts and their directors. Near the front of the wooden part of the main deck are the two wildcats: the capstan heads that operated the anchor chains. To the sides of the wildcats are two smaller capstans. *Naval History and Heritage Command*

The *Wisconsin*, from the forward 40-mm gun mounts to the aft smokestack, is viewed from the upper port quarter while in AFDB-1 at Guam in April 1952. The antennas on the foremast are discernible. On the rounded platform on the foretop is the SPS-6 air-search radar. To the upper rear of that antenna, on a stub mast, is an SG-6 surface-search radar antenna. Just aft of the SG-6 antenna is another stub mast, with radio antennas. *Naval History and Heritage Command*

An above-the-stern aerial photo shows USS *Wisconsin* docked in the fully floated AFDB-1 at Guam in early April 1952. This feat represented the successful floating of the largest ship to date in a floating drydock. *US Navy*

USS *Wisconsin* is observed off her starboard bow while ensconced in USS AFDB-1, at Apra Harbor, Guam, on April 5, 1952. As seen in the photo, the floating drydock was not large enough to accommodate the entire battleship, the bow of which protruded from the front of the drydock. *Naval History and Heritage Command*

Another April 5, 1952, photograph depicts the *Wisconsin* from astern while docked in AFDB-1 at Apra, Guam. The four propellers are visible: four-bladed ones on the outboard shafts, and five-bladed propellers inboard. The floating drydock's designation and the letter assigned to its aft section, "J," are on the rear of the starboard wing wall. *Naval History and Heritage Command*

The two rudders and the four propellers of the *Wisconsin* are in view in this photo taken from the floor of AFDB-1 at Guam in April 1952. The two outboard propellers each had four blades, while the inboard propellers had five blades. *George Penning via USS* Wisconsin *Association*

USS AFDB-1 with USS *Wisconsin* docked inside is viewed from the port side at Apra Harbor, Guam, on April 5, 1952. Another floating drydock is visible across the harbor, in the left background. *Naval History and Heritage Command*

1950s SERVICE 79

Several changes are evident in this photo of USS *Wisconsin* cruising off the coast of Korea on March 2, 1954. A larger ship's number, a white "64" with black shadowing, has been painted on the bow. The rangefinder has been removed from turret 1. The mainmast to the rear of the aft smokestack has been replaced by a bulkier one of quadropod design. Mounted on the top of the new mainmast was an AN/SPS-8 height-finding radar antenna. *US Navy*

After being relieved of duty in the West Pacific in April 1954, the *Wisconsin* returned to the United States. In the last half of April of that year, the ship is transiting the Panama Canal; the view is to the port side of turret 2; turret 1 is to the far right. On May 4, the *Wisconsin* arrived at its new base, at Norfolk, Virginia. *R. Zinkan via USS Wisconsin Association*

USS *Wisconsin* is negotiating one of the locks of the Panama Canal in late April 1954. The view was taken from the aft starboard corner of the 02 level, with the side of turret 3 in the foreground. Note the left rangefinder hood, the toe rail around the turret roof, and the beam on the edge of the turret roof for lowering 16-inch shells belowdecks. On the deck to the left of the rangefinder hood is a winch. *Dom Menta via USS Wisconsin Association*

USS *Wisconsin* tied up in New York prior to sailing to Europe. A signboard has been hung on the bow reading "USS *Wisconsin*, BB-64." *Dom Menta via USS* Wisconsin *Association*

During a summer cruise to Europe in 1955, USS *Wisconsin* paid a call to the port of Edinburgh, Scotland, from July 26 to August 1. Here, crewmen of the battleship watch as Scottish bagpipers and drummers assemble on the deck, to welcome the ship to the port. *Dom Menta via USS* Wisconsin *Association*

Sailors and Marines of USS *Wisconsin* observe the proceedings as the port of Edinburgh welcomes the battleship on or around July 26, 1955. Note the two officers standing on the stored boat in the right background. *Dom Menta via USS* Wisconsin *Association*

While in transit from the shipyard at Bayonne, New Jersey, to the Brooklyn Navy Yard on October 18 1955, USS *Wisconsin* ran aground on Diamond Reef, midway between Governor's Island and the southern tip of Manhattan. Tugboats freed the *Wisconsin* in forty-five minutes. The battleship is seen here later on that day, just passing under the Manhattan Bridge, as it made its way up the East River. In the background is the Brooklyn Bridge. *Dom Menta via USS* Wisconsin *Association*

1950s SERVICE 81

The *Wisconsin* suffered heavy damage to its bow, and the *Eaton*, as seen here, suffered a large gash in its hull to the front of the superstructure. Only one crewman of the *Eaton* was injured. *Dom Menta via USS* Wisconsin *Association*

USS *Eaton* is under tow by the boat to the left after the collision with USS *Wisconsin*. The collision fractured the *Eaton*'s keel. The destroyer's crew secured it by reinforcing the hull structure with anchor chain from the bow to the stern. *Dom Menta via USS* Wisconsin *Association*

Crewmen of the *Wisconsin* survey the damage to the foredeck following the collision with USS *Eaton* on May 6, 1956. The force of the collision caused steel deck plates in the foreground to warp and buckle. *Dom Menta via USS* Wisconsin *Association*

USS *Wisconsin* tied up in New York prior to sailing to Europe. A signboard has been hung on the bow reading "USS *Wisconsin*, BB-64." *Dom Menta via USS* Wisconsin *Association*

During a summer cruise to Europe in 1955, USS *Wisconsin* paid a call to the port of Edinburgh, Scotland, from July 26 to August 1. Here, crewmen of the battleship watch as Scottish bagpipers and drummers assemble on the deck, to welcome the ship to the port. *Dom Menta via USS* Wisconsin *Association*

Sailors and Marines of USS *Wisconsin* observe the proceedings as the port of Edinburgh welcomes the battleship on or around July 26, 1955. Note the two officers standing on the stored boat in the right background. *Dom Menta via USS* Wisconsin *Association*

While in transit from the shipyard at Bayonne, New Jersey, to the Brooklyn Navy Yard on October 18 1955, USS *Wisconsin* ran aground on Diamond Reef, midway between Governor's Island and the southern tip of Manhattan. Tugboats freed the *Wisconsin* in forty-five minutes. The battleship is seen here later on that day, just passing under the Manhattan Bridge, as it made its way up the East River. In the background is the Brooklyn Bridge. *Dom Menta via USS* Wisconsin *Association*

1950s SERVICE 81

As seen in a January 22, 1956, photograph of USS *Wisconsin*, the aircraft crane has now been removed, and two king posts to the rear of the aft smokestack now are supporting both the two rear legs of the mainmast and boat booms. The port boat boom is visible next to the aft smokestack. *US Navy*

On the same date the preceding photo was taken, this aerial view of the *Wisconsin* was taken from above the starboard side. Two motorboats are stacked, one above the other, alongside the rear of the superstructure, and several more boats are stored on the main deck aft of turret 3. During peacetime, many odd items of cargo could be found on the decks of USN battleships; a four-wheeled truck is parked below the left 16-inch/50-caliber gun of turret 3. Spotted on the aft part of the main deck is a Piasecki HUP Retriever helicopter. *US Navy*

Anchored at Guantánamo Bay, Cuba, the *Wisconsin* is in full dress, fore and aft, in honor of George Washington's birthday, on February 22, 1956. *US Navy*

While operating at 20 knots in heavy fog in the Atlantic off the Virginia Capes on the afternoon of May 6, 1956, USS *Wisconsin* collided with the starboard side of the destroyer USS *Eaton* (DDE-510). The heavily damaged destroyer is seen from the forward part of the main deck of the *Wisconsin*, not long after the collision. *Dom Menta via USS* Wisconsin *Association*

As seen from the *Wisconsin*, the collision destroyed the forward part of the superstructure, the forward 5-inch gun mount, and the RUR-4 Weapon Alpha antisubmarine missile launcher. *Dom Menta via USS* Wisconsin *Association*

1950s SERVICE 83

The *Wisconsin* suffered heavy damage to its bow, and the *Eaton*, as seen here, suffered a large gash in its hull to the front of the superstructure. Only one crewman of the *Eaton* was injured. *Dom Menta via USS* Wisconsin *Association*

USS *Eaton* is under tow by the boat to the left after the collision with USS *Wisconsin*. The collision fractured the *Eaton*'s keel. The destroyer's crew secured it by reinforcing the hull structure with anchor chain from the bow to the stern. *Dom Menta via USS* Wisconsin *Association*

Crewmen of the *Wisconsin* survey the damage to the foredeck following the collision with USS *Eaton* on May 6, 1956. The force of the collision caused steel deck plates in the foreground to warp and buckle. *Dom Menta via USS* Wisconsin *Association*

The damage to the bow of the *Wisconsin* from its collision with the destroyer *Eaton* is evident in this view facing aft. A large section of the bow was ripped open but still hung onto the side of the hull. *Naval History and Heritage Command*

A crewman holds a folding rule over a warped section of foredeck on the *Wisconsin*. Nonslip strips are on this part of the deck. *Dom Menta via USS* Wisconsin *Association*

In another photo taken shortly after the collision between the *Wisconsin* and the *Eaton*, two crewmen of the battleship, including the one in the preceding photo, are holding a folding rule over a section of diamond-tread steel plate that buckled as a result of the collision. *Dom Menta via USS* Wisconsin *Association*

After the collision with the *Eaton*, the *Wisconsin* proceeded to Norfolk, Virginia, for repairs. The battleship is being moored to a dock there, with the assistance of a tugboat. In the left background is *Wisconsin*'s sister ship USS *New Jersey* (BB-62). *National Archives*

The torn bow of the *Wisconsin* is viewed from the aft starboard quarter at Norfolk. In addition to the large rent in the bow, the collision with the *Eaton* caused warping and rippling of the steel on the main deck as well as on the side of the bow. On the starboard side, a vertical kink is visible on the side of the bow, in line with the number "6." *Dom Menta via USS Wisconsin Association*

The rip in *Wisconsin*'s bow is seen from slightly forward on the port side. In the background is the bow of USS *New Jersey*. *Robert Klotz via USS* Wisconsin *Association*

The damaged bow of the *Wisconsin* is seen from aft on the starboard side while docked at Norfolk. *Robert Klotz via USS* Wisconsin *Association*

A week after the collision with the *Eaton*, the *Wisconsin* was placed in drydock at Norfolk for repairs. Here, the damaged bow has been removed from the hull and is being hoisted away. *Robert Klotz via USS Wisconsin Association*

To expedite repairs to the bow of the *Wisconsin*, the bow of its unfinished sister ship, the Iowa-class battleship *Kentucky*, was cannibalized and grafted onto the *Wisconsin*. At that time, the *Kentucky* was in storage at the Newport News Shipbuilding and Dry Dock Company, across Hampton Roads from Norfolk. The hull of the *Kentucky* is seen here from the port side, being towed at Norfolk Navy Yard in January 1950. *National Archives*

The unfinished battleship *Kentucky* is seen in an undated aerial view before its bow was removed. The ship was constructed at the Norfolk Navy Yard. Work on the ship was suspended in February 1947, by which time the construction had been completed to the second deck. Conical shelters were over the barbettes for the three 16-inch/50-caliber turrets. *National Archives*

On May 17, 1956, the hull of the *Kentucky* is entering a drydock at the Newport News Shipbuilding and Dry Dock Company, where the bow will be removed and transferred for grafting onto USS *Wisconsin*. Since the preceding photo of the hull was taken, at least six gunhouses for twin 5-inch/38-caliber gun mounts had been placed on the starboard side of the second deck.

After the bow was removed from the *Kentucky*, the entire bow assembly was transported by a crane barge across Hampton Roads to the Norfolk Navy Yard, for installation on the *Wisconsin*. The process to graft the bow onto the *Wisconsin* took sixteen days, with workers operating around the clock. The battleship returned to seaworthy condition on June 28, 1956. *National Archives*

Less than two weeks after repairs on the bow of the *Wisconsin* were completed, the battleship embarked 700 midshipmen of the Naval Reserve Officers Training Corps (NROTC) for a summer training cruise. The ship is seen here during the course of this cruise, which included visits to Barcelona, Spain; Greenock, Scotland; and Guantánamo Bay, Cuba. *Robert Klotz via USS* Wisconsin *Association*

On Good Friday, April 19, 1957, a Roman Catholic mass is being conducted on the fantail of USS *Wisconsin* while anchored at Naples, Italy. The ship had arrived in that port the preceding day. During that month, *Wisconsin* and crew participated in a NATO operation, Red Pivot, in the Mediterranean. *Robert Klotz via USS* Wisconsin *Association*

On November 5, 1957, folding chairs are arrayed on the foredeck of the *Wisconsin*, moored alongside Pier 86 on the North River in Manhattan. The chairs were for seating attendees at a ceremony celebrating the *Wisconsin*'s status as the last commissioned battleship at that time, as well as the impending end of its second in-commission career. A few days later the ship would proceed to nearby Bayonne, New Jersey, where it would be prepared for long-term storage. *Boyd Hancock via USS* Wisconsin *Association*

Lt. (j.g.) Charles T. Denner, assigned to USS *Wisconsin* for the preceding nineteen months, salutes the battleship upon his departure from the ship following its decommissioning ceremony at Bayonne, New Jersey, on March 8, 1958. This marked the first time the US Navy did not have a battleship in commission since 1895.

Following its decommissioning in March 1958, the *Wisconsin* has been prepared for long-term storage at its berth at Bayonne, New Jersey. As seen from the forecastle, yellowish sealing material has been installed between the barrels of the 16-inch guns and the fronts of the turrets, to keep out the elements. Similarly, yellow material has been placed over the glass on the navigating bridge and on other areas of the superstructure where water could get in. *Boyd Hancock via USS Wisconsin Association*

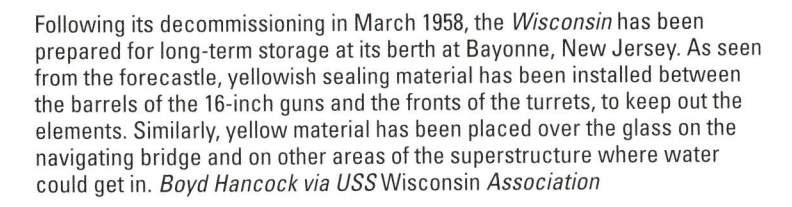

More of the yellow sealing material is visible in this photo of the *Wisconsin* from the fantail, facing forward. An "igloo" structure is to the right. Towering above the aft Mk. 38 main-battery director are the two king posts for the boat cranes, which also helped support the mainmast. *Boyd Hancock via USS Wisconsin Association*

1950s SERVICE 93

CHAPTER 4
The Long Rest

In August 1962, after about four and a half years in mothballs at Bayonne, the *Wisconsin* was relocated to the Philadelphia Navy Yard. The battleship is seen here at the beginning of its journey, on August 8, as it crosses New York Harbor, heading south, assisted by tugboats.

Wisconsin remained tied up as part of the Reserve Fleet in Bayonne until 1962, when the Bayonne facility was slated for closing. On August 17, it was towed to the reserve facility in Philadelphia.

When *Wisconsin* was placed in reserve in 1958, it joined fourteen other battleships already placed in reserve. Sister ships *Missouri*, *New Jersey*, and *Iowa* had been laid up in 1955, 1957, and February 1958, respectively. Also in reserve were the four South Dakota–class ships, both North Carolina–class ships, the three Colorado-class ships, and both Tennessee-class ships.

As the years passed, the older battleships were stricken from the Navy list and sold for scrap or offered as donations as veterans' memorials. *Tennessee* and *California*, as well as *Maryland*, *Colorado*, and *West Virginia*, were stricken in March 1959, and shortly thereafter all were reduced to scrap. *Washington* followed suit in June 1960, while its sister *North Carolina* was saved as a memorial. By the time the *South Dakota*s were stricken in June 1962, interest in preservation had increased, and two of the four became monuments, with *Indiana* and *South Dakota* itself succumbing to the scrapper's torch.

With the devastating effect of its 16-inch gunfire on the enemy in Korea still relatively fresh in the military mind, discarding the battleship out of hand was not considered.

During this time, however, various proposals were brought forth to convert the *Iowa*s to other configurations, ranging from guided-missile launch ships to combination aircraft carrier and surface combatant, or even possibly a combination fast combat support ship with bombardment capability.

The war in Vietnam brought about the reactivation of its sister *New Jersey* in April 1968. During the *New Jersey*'s reactivation by Philadelphia Naval Shipyard, the *Wisconsin* was found to be a ready source of spare parts. This cannibalization was one of the reasons that *Wisconsin* would be the last of the Iowa-class ships reactivated decades later.

In 1967, the four Iowa-class battleships were the only battleships still remaining in the US Navy's Reserve Fleet. Three of these ships were in storage at Philadelphia Navy Yard; they are, *left to right*, *Wisconsin* (BB-64), *New Jersey* (BB-62), and *Iowa* (BB-61). The fourth ship, *Missouri* (BB-63), was in storage at Bremerton, Washington. *National Archives*

The *Wisconsin*, *center*, is being towed from a nest of battleships at a dock at the Philadelphia Navy Yard in June 1967. The other two battleships are the *New Jersey* and *Iowa*. The reason for moving the *Wisconsin* was to enable the *New Jersey*, which was being reactivated for service in the Vietnam War, to be towed from the nest. *National Archives*

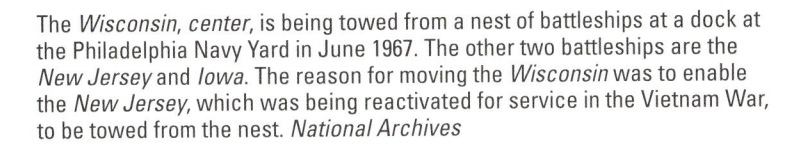

The *Wisconsin* was still in long-term storage at Philadelphia Naval Yard when this aerial photo was taken in 1978. That battleship is nested in the foreground between the Essex-class carrier *Shangri-La* (CV-38), *right*, and the battleship *Iowa*, *left*. *National Archives*

THE LONG REST 95

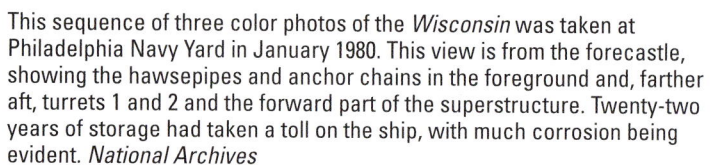

This sequence of three color photos of the *Wisconsin* was taken at Philadelphia Navy Yard in January 1980. This view is from the forecastle, showing the hawsepipes and anchor chains in the foreground and, farther aft, turrets 1 and 2 and the forward part of the superstructure. Twenty-two years of storage had taken a toll on the ship, with much corrosion being evident. *National Archives*

The barrel of the right 16-inch/50-caliber gun of turret 1 is observed close-up. Note the cover over the muzzle and the heavy rust on the plugs between the gun barrels and the front of the turret. *National Museum of the US Navy*

Visible in this view are several of the twin 5-inch/38-caliber gun mounts on the battleships *Wisconsin* and *Iowa* in January 1980. Heavy rust on steel surfaces and deteriorated planks on the decks were prevalent. *National Museum of the US Navy*

By the time this photograph was taken at Philadelphia in 1984, the battleship *Wisconsin* had been in long-term storage in the Reserve Fleet for twenty-six years. The photo was taken off the starboard beam, with the aft Mk. 38 main-battery director (with radar removed), the boat cranes, the mainmast, and the aft smokestack in the foreground. *A. D. Baker III*

THE LONG REST 97

CHAPTER 5
Return to Service

During the 1970s, the tide began to turn against the venerable battleships, and many forces from within and outside the US Navy sought to have them stricken and set for disposal. Variously, Secretary of the Navy John Warner, or Chief of Naval Operations Elmo Zumwalt, or more often the Marines, who fondly recalled the effectiveness of heavy naval gunfire during amphibious operations, forced the *Iowa*s to be maintained in the reserve fleet.

During the closing years of the Carter administration, momentum began to grow in naval circles and Congress to reactivate the *Iowa*s, in large part due to the buildup of the Soviet navy and increased Soviet aggression. Feeling that such reactivation would undermine peace efforts, the administration blocked all such efforts. The election of Ronald Reagan to the nation's highest office not only removed the biggest hurdle from the reactivation efforts but also brought with it a new champion for the cause in the form of the new secretary of the Navy, John F. Lehman Jr.

While the most recently used *New Jersey* would be the first to be reactivated, with the first money for the project budgeted in 1981, *Iowa* would be next, with the long lead money budgeted in fiscal year 1982, followed by *Missouri* in 1986.

Unlike the previous recommissionings of the ships, this time extensive work was done. The boilers were converted to burn diesel fuel marine (DFM) rather than bunker oil, a sewage collection system was installed, extensive revisions were made to the electronics suite, and, significantly, four of the 5-inch, 38-caliber dual-purpose mounts were removed, making way for installation of thirty-two long-range Tomahawk cruise missiles in armored box launchers. Also included in the refit were sixteen Harpoon medium-range missiles and four close-in weapons systems (CIWS) to protect the vessel from missile or aircraft attack. Importantly for the crew, air conditioning was added to the vessels.

During February 1986, preliminary work to recommission the *Wisconsin* was done at the Philadelphia Naval Shipyard. The vessel was then towed to the Avondale shipyard in New Orleans on August 1 for hull cleaning and repair, and then on to Ingalls Shipbuilding in Pascagoula, Mississippi, for extensive modification.

On October 22, 1988, USS *Wisconsin* was recommissioned in Pascagoula, with Capt. Jerry Morgan Blesch commanding. For the next several months the battleship operated off Norfolk and in the Gulf of Mexico, but on August 2, 1990, world events moved it to another gulf.

The Iraqi invasion of Kuwait brought about a worldwide military response. On August 7, *Wisconsin* stood out from Norfolk, steaming for the Persian Gulf, making the 8,500 miles in sixteen days.

For four months the *Wisconsin* did in the Persian Gulf much as it had in the Pacific thirty-five years earlier—its crew drilled and it refueled smaller ships and provided medical and dental care for crews of smaller vessels, as well as using its expansive repair shops to maintain the lesser ships.

However, *Wisconsin* also served as the command ship for Tomahawk cruise missile strike warfare. It ordered the launch by the destroyer *Paul F. Foster* of the first of the Tomahawk launches at 0140:20 on January 17, 1991, which was quickly followed by forty-six more missiles in the initial volley, including eight of *Wisconsin*'s own.

On February 6, *Wisconsin* relieved its sister ship *Missouri* on the gun line near the Kuwait border. Almost immediately a USMC OV-10 Bronco aircraft called for a fire mission. *Wisconsin* responded by placing eleven rounds on an Iraqi artillery battery. The next morning, twenty-nine more big rounds were dispatched toward an Iraqi communications facility. That evening the 16-inch rifles turned their attention to nautical enemies, targeting Iraqi Special Forces boats on the Kuwaiti coast. Fifty massive high-explosive rounds made short work of the small craft and associated piers and facilities.

The ship's targeting equipment was augmented by remotely piloted vehicles (RPVs), drone aircraft flown from the battlewagon's afterdeck.

In the following days, the battleship's big guns smothered numerous enemy targets, to the extent that the enemy became so wary of the thunderous explosions that often followed the buzz of the RPV that on March 1, a number of Iraqi soldiers waved white flags of surrender to the drone, rather than face the aftermath of being spotted.

Wisconsin left the northern Persian Gulf on March 4, 1991, steaming toward Norfolk, after having expended 528 16-inch rounds and 881 5-inch rounds in answering thirty-six calls for naval gunfire support, in addition to launching twenty-five Tomahawk cruise missiles.

Just as had been the case with the *New Jersey* operating off Vietnam decades earlier, despite the stellar performance of *Wisconsin* the chief of naval operations ordered the battleship decommissioned by the end of 1991. That order was carried out, and the *Wisconsin* was decommissioned for the final time on September 30, 1991.

Following twenty-eight years on the inactive rolls, the Navy began preparations to modernize and recommission *Wisconsin* under a program to greatly strengthen its surface forces. The battleship would be fully refurbished and equipped with state-of-the-art technology and weaponry. The work would be carried out at the Avondale Shipyard, at New Orleans, and at Ingalls Shipbuilding, Pascagoula, Mississippi. Here, the *Wisconsin* is under tow in August 1986 during transit to the southern shipyards. Note that the Mk. 38 directors have been removed, and the shields of the twin 5-inch/38-caliber gun mounts have been dismounted and are resting on the main deck adjacent to turrets 2 and 3. *US Navy*

Scaffolding and staging have been erected on the battleship *Wisconsin* at Ingalls Shipbuilding in Pascagoula, in September 1987, and the work of modernizing the ship is well underway. By now, the wooden planks of the main deck have been removed, exposing the steel deck underneath. The 40 mm gun platform and splinter shield finally have been permanently removed from the roof of turret 2, and turret 3 would receive the same treatment. *US Navy*

RETURN TO SERVICE 99

The superstructure and forward smokestack of the *Wisconsin* are encased in scaffolding during the modernization work at Ingalls Shipbuilding, Pascagoula, on September 17, 1987. The cylindrical structures aft of the conning tower and abeam the forward smokestack are the foundations for Mk. 37 secondary-battery directors, which have been dismounted. According to the original label of this photograph, the overhaul of the ship was 50 percent complete by this date. *US Navy*

Workmen at Ingalls Shipyard are fastening teak planks to the main deck. The edges and ends of the planks were rabbeted, to allow space for caulking between the installed planks. *US Navy*

Several new features have been installed on the *Wisconsin* in this September 1987 photo at Ingalls Shipyard. On the foredeck is the antenna array for the Naval Tactical Data System (NTDS), for acquiring targets and selecting weapons. The newly reinstalled forward Mk. 38 director atop the superstructure has been mounted on a new, box-shaped compartment containing the AN/SLQ-32(V)3 electronic-countermeasures (ECM) system. *US Navy*

Following its overhaul and modernization work, the *Wisconsin* underwent a series of sea trials in the summer of 1988, in advance of its recommissioning later that year. The refurbished battleship is seen here leaving port with the assistance of a tugboat at its stern. During the recent overhaul, the mainmast had been removed. The black-painted foremast supported, *from front to rear*, the SPS-67 short-range tactical surface and low air-search antenna, the much-larger SPS-49 long-range air-search radar antenna, and the tower-shaped TACAN (tactical air navigation) antenna. *US Navy*

In an aerial view taken off *Wisconsin*'s port stern on August 30, 1988, the battleship is proceeding under its own power for the first time since its decommissioning, in March 1956. The crane-shaped structure adjacent to the aft-starboard portion of the superstructure is the outrigger for the newly installed underway replenishment (UNREP) system. The outrigger served to manage fuel lines used in underway refueling operations. *US Navy*

In a photograph likely taken in the final days of August 1988, the 16-inch/50-caliber guns of the *Wisconsin* are being test-fired in the Gulf of Mexico. To each side of the superstructure above the pilothouse are white, cylindrical objects with domes on the tops. These are part of the Mk. 15 20 mm Phalanx CIWS (close-in weapons system). Four of them were installed on the ship during its modernization. These weapons were designed to track and shoot down close-in threats to the ship, such as helicopters and antiship missiles. *US Navy*

At Ingalls Shipyard, Pascagoula, Mississippi, the *Wisconsin* is dressed fore to aft on October 22, 1988, the date of its recommissioning ceremony, at which time the ship was returned to active service with the US Navy. Greatly augmenting the ship's 16-inch/50-caliber guns were two new missile systems: sixteen AGM-84 Harpoon antiship missiles were installed, along with eight armored box launcher (ABL) mounts containing thirty-two BGM-109 Tomahawk cruise missiles. *US Navy*

Members of USS *Wisconsin*'s recommissioning crew are hustling up the gangways to the main deck of the battleship just before the recommissioning ceremony on October 22, 1988. *US Navy*

Guests throng the dock at the recommissioning ceremony for USS *Wisconsin*. Some 12,000 persons attended the ceremony. *US Navy*

In the interval since the preceding photo was taken, the crew of the *Wisconsin* have manned the rails of the main deck and all levels of the superstructure, and the 16-inch/50-caliber guns have been trained to port. Atop the forward Mk. 37 director, above and aft of the pilothouse, is the dish antenna for the Mk. 25 radar. *US Navy*

While docked at Norfolk, Virginia, in December 1989, USS *Wisconsin* is decorated for the holidays, including lights fore and aft and a Christmas tree on the roof of turret 2. *US Navy*

USS *Wisconsin* once again saw action in the early 1990s, in the First Gulf War. The battleship departed from Norfolk on August 7, 1990, five days after Iraqi forces invaded Kuwait, precipitating the war. Sixteen days later, after a transit of 8,500 miles, the battleship arrived at its station in the Persian Gulf, ready for combat operations. In the gulf during the early part of Operation Desert Shield (the buildup and "defense of Saudi Arabia" phase of the war), on September 1, 1990, Gen. Colin L. Powell, chairman of the Joint Chiefs of Staff, stands on one of the anchor wildcats, *left of center*, as he addresses members of the crew of the *Wisconsin*. *US Navy*

104 USS WISCONSIN (BB-64)

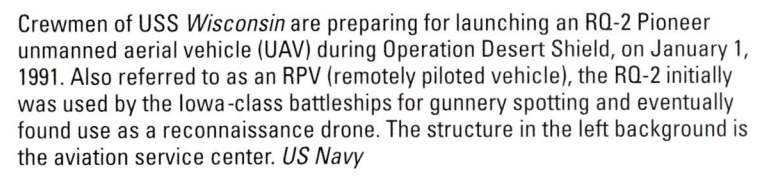

Crewmen of USS *Wisconsin* are preparing for launching an RQ-2 Pioneer unmanned aerial vehicle (UAV) during Operation Desert Shield, on January 1, 1991. Also referred to as an RPV (remotely piloted vehicle), the RQ-2 initially was used by the Iowa-class battleships for gunnery spotting and eventually found use as a reconnaissance drone. The structure in the left background is the aviation service center. *US Navy*

An RQ-2 Pioneer UAV takes off from the *Wisconsin* during Operation Desert Shield. The drone was powered by a propeller driven by a Sachs two-stroke, two-cylinder engine, but takeoff was achieved with RATO (rocket-assisted takeoff). *US Navy*

As viewed facing aft from the roof of turret 3 of USS *Wisconsin*, an RQ-2 Pioneer has just been retrieved by flying it into a net rigged to poles aft of the turret. *US Navy*

RETURN TO SERVICE 105

Sister ships USS *Wisconsin*, left, and USS *Missouri* are operating together in the Persian Gulf during Operation Desert Shield, on January 1, 1991. The white shape in the background beyond turret 2 of the *Wisconsin* is part of the hospital ship USNS *Comfort* (T-AH-20). *US Navy*

By the time of the First Gulf War, the *Wisconsin* was equipped with a nuclear-biological-chemical (NBC) countermeasure water wash-down system, to remove contaminants should the ship be exposed to an enemy NBC attack. That system is being tested aboard the *Wisconsin* four days after the start of Operation Desert Storm, the combat phase of the war, on January 22, 1991. In the foreground is the support frame for the NTDS antenna, as well as the lower part of the antenna. *US Navy*

A BGM-109 Tomahawk land-attack missile (TLAM) has just been launched from a Mk. 143 armored box launcher (ABL) aboard USS *Wisconsin* (BB-64) during Operation Desert Storm, in January 1991. The Tomahawk was a long-range, all-weather, subsonic cruise missile capable of carrying conventional or nuclear payloads. The US Navy fired a total of 288 Tomahawk cruise missiles at Iraqi targets during the First Gulf War. *US Navy*

In another view of the launching of a Tomahawk cruise missile from USS *Wisconsin* during Operation Desert Storm, the nose of the missile is faintly visible at the upper center of the photo. To the left are two Harpoon antiship missile launchers, each with four launching tubes. *US Navy*

A little more than 2½ Iowa-class battleships can be seen in this photo! In the center, between battleships USS *Missouri*, foreground, and the USS *Wisconsin*, is the fast combat support ship USS *Sacramento* (AOE-1). *Sacramento* was powered by two of the four power plants that were manufactured for installation on USS *Kentucky* (BB-66). The other half of *Kentucky*'s power plant went into *Sacramento*'s sister ship, *Camden* (AOE-2). *Sacramento* was commissioned in 1964, about twenty years after the engineering equipment was manufactured. Note the difference in the ships' numbers on the bows of the two battleships: all black for *Missouri* and white with black shadowing on *Wisconsin*, at the time of this January 1991 underway replenishment (UNREP) during the First Gulf War. *US Navy*

Crewmen of USS *Wisconsin* are steadying pallets of 5-inch/38-caliber shells as they arrive during an UNREP from USS *Sacramento* during the First Gulf War in 1991. Cages over the tops of the shells keep them from shifting around during transit. *US Navy*

The right 16-inch/50-caliber gun of turret 1 has just fired a round at an Iraqi target during a shore bombardment in February 1991. In the foreground is a pedestal-mounted Browning M2HB .50-caliber machine gun, for close-in defense against targets such as boats or helicopters. *US Navy*

Another photo of turret 1 firing at Iraqi forces on the shore in Kuwait in February 1991 includes a good view of the layout of the front of the superstructure at that time. The bulbous feature just below the ECM compartment was the housing for the RPV (remotely piloted vehicle) guidance antenna, added between December 1989 and September 1990. On each side of the roof of the ECM compartment is a box-shaped pod with ECM sensors and antennas. *US Navy*

RETURN TO SERVICE 109

The right 16-inch/50-caliber gun of turret 2 of USS *Wisconsin* is firing to starboard while underway on May 28, 1991. This represented the final firing of the battleship's big guns before it was decommissioned for the final time in September of that year. *US Navy*

On June 6, 1991, crewmen of USS *Wisconsin* in dress whites line the rails as a harbor tug sprays water by way of welcome to New York's Victory Celebration. The daylong event honored the Coalition forces that liberated Kuwait during Operation Desert Storm. *USMC*

USS *Wisconsin* was decommissioned for the third and last time on September 30, 1991, this time at Norfolk, Virginia. Here, crew members man the rails during the battleship's decommissioning ceremony. Much equipment and materiel had already been removed from the ship, causing it to ride high in the water. *US Navy*

Crew members of the *Wisconsin* are disembarking from the battleship for the final time during the decommissioning ceremony at Norfolk on September 30, 1991. The massive foremast and its radar antennas had been removed. *US Navy*

While in storage at the Philadelphia Naval Shipyard, the *Wisconsin* was stricken from the Naval Vessel Register on January 12, 1995. One year and nine months later, on October 15, 1996, the battleship was towed from Philadelphia to the Norfolk Naval Shipyard. The *Wisconsin* is shown during that journey, shorn of much of its exterior equipment, including rigging and antennas. A box-shaped shelter is present over the forward Mk. 37 director atop the superstructure. *US Navy*

CHAPTER 6
Museum Ship

Following almost a decade in long-term storage at Philadelphia Naval Shipyard after its decommissioning, the battleship *Wisconsin* was given a new lease on life as a museum ship, permanently moored at the Nauticus and Naval Heritage Museum, in Hampton Roads, Virginia. This aerial photo depicts the *Wisconsin* at its berth at the museum on January 20, 2001. *US Navy*

After decommissioning, *Wisconsin* was towed to Philadelphia to be laid up once more in the shipyard that gave birth to it, and where it had been previously laid up from August 1962 until August 1986. However, five years later, when the Philadelphia Navy Yard closed in October 1996, *Wisconsin* was towed back to Norfolk.

During this time it was struck from the Navy list on January 12, 1995. The 1999 Strom Thurmond National Defense Authorization Act required that the *Iowa* and *Wisconsin* be returned to the Navy list. Accordingly, it returned to the Naval Vessel Register on February 12, 1998. This was done to pave the way for donation of the *New Jersey*, which had been maintained in reserve, for use as a memorial.

Wisconsin, too big to reach its namesake state, would find a fitting new home in Norfolk, frequently its home port as well as the home of the US Navy's largest installation.

An agreement was reached with the USS *Wisconsin* Foundation to move the battleship into a position adjacent to the Nauticus Museum in downtown Norfolk and to open its weather decks for display, while not altering the ship and still maintaining the state of preservation of interior spaces and weapons. The ship would thus be displayed in a manner similar to that which USS *Missouri* had been displayed in Bremerton, Washington, from the 1950s until it, like *Wisconsin*, was reactivated under the Reagan administration. The weather decks of the *Wisconsin* opened for tourists on April 16, 2001.

In 2006, the secretary of the Navy again struck *Wisconsin* (and *Iowa*) from the Navy list, and shortly thereafter Congress passed the National Defense Act of 2006, which, at the insistence of Sen. John Warner, mandated that the *Iowa* and *Wisconsin* be kept and maintained in a state of readiness and able to be returned to service. As a practical matter, what this meant was that the Navy continued to pay to maintain the huge ships.

On December 14, 2009, *Wisconsin*'s years of Navy service came to a close when the government donated the veteran battleship to the City of Norfolk.

That donation, however, came with interesting "strings." First, the city was required to use and maintain impressed cathodic protection and dehumidification systems where necessary to control corrosion. This would prevent the *Wisconsin* from suffering severe hull deterioration, as had been the case with USS *Texas*, USS *Olympia*, and, to a lesser extent, USS *North Carolina*.

This "string" was undoubtedly tied to the other one, paragraph 2, subparagraph d, which read: "Any alterations of the Vessel must preserve the capability of being reverted by the Navy, in the event the Navy requests the Donee return the Vessel in case of national emergency." The paragraph goes on to specify that changes must be able to be reversed in a shipyard in less than three days.

Immediately after this transfer, gradual work began to open increasing amounts of *Wisconsin*'s interior spaces to visitors. This work is ongoing as of this writing.

The battleship *Wisconsin* presents a graceful bow at its berth at Nauticus. Around the upper front of the bulwark of the forecastle is a venturi windscreen, a metal structure that channeled the wind upward, sparing the occupants of the forecastle from strong breezes. Below the center of the bulwark is the bullnose, and to the sides are the two anchors.

The ship's number on the port side is shown. The black area at the bottom is the boot topping: a special treatment that masked the oily deposits that usually collected along the ship's waterline while in harbors.

The *Wisconsin* during its residence at Nauticus has been maintained in a high state of preservation, largely mimicking its appearance and configuration during its 1988–91 period of active service. The battleship is seen here from off its port bow.

MUSEUM SHIP 115

The wildcats, with white crossed anchors on the tops, are in the foreground, as seen from the forecastle of the *Wisconsin*. To the immediate rear of the wildcats are the horizontally oriented handwheels for the wildcats; a control wheel is on each outboard side, and two brake handwheels are in the center.

A view from the dock at Nauticus incorporates much of the starboard side of the *Wisconsin*, from turret 2 (*to the far right*) to the superstructure, mainmast, smokestacks, and two of the twin 5-inch/38-caliber gun mounts. Jutting from the front of the enclosed navigating bridge are two whip antennas.

The starboard side and the front of the enclosed navigating bridge are viewed. The pilothouse, also designated the secondary conning station, is inside the enclosed bridge, in the next-from-top level of the heavily armored conning tower. The primary conning station of the ship was partway up the front of the forward fire-control tower, part of the upper forward extension of the superstructure. The top of the conning tower is visible above the navigating bridge; this contained the fire-control station. To the upper rear of the top of the conning tower is the forward Mk. 37 secondary-battery director, with the right objective of its rangefinder jutting from its side.

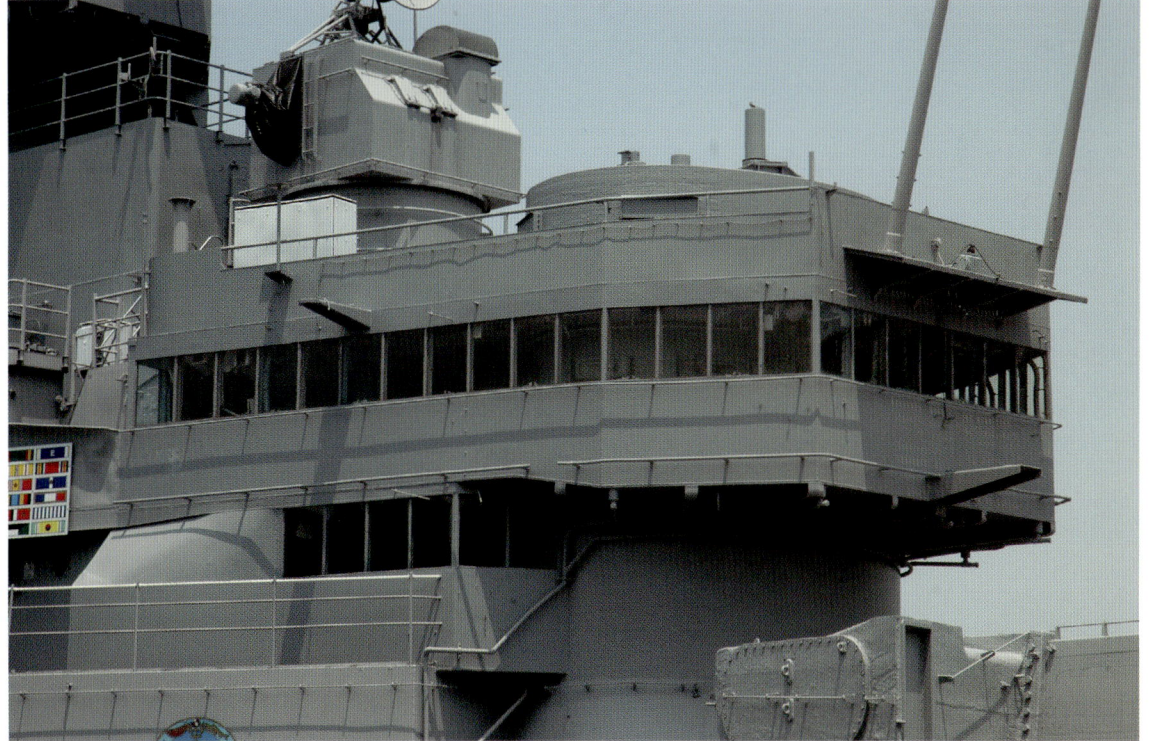

MUSEUM SHIP 117

In a view from the forward fire-control tower, at the bottom are the Mk. 25 dish antenna for the forward Mk. 37 director, the roof of the conning tower, and the open bridge. Farther forward are the roofs and the gun barrels of turrets 1 and 2.

From a lower level of the forward fire-control tower than in the preceding photo, the forward Mk. 37 director and its Mk. 25 dish antenna are viewed from aft. Note the black boot where the left objective of the rangefinder of the director enters the side of the director's armored shield.

The NTDS antenna array over the foredeck of the *Wisconsin* is seen from aft. This system collected data from various ships in the battle force to arrive at a unified map of the battle space. On the rear of the antenna support platform is a ship's bell.

MUSEUM SHIP 119

The aft part of the *Wisconsin* is viewed from the front of the forward smokestack, showing part of the mainmast's support structure in the foreground. Visible below are four of the ship's eight armored box launcher (ABL) mounts, each of which held four BGM-109 Tomahawk cruise missiles.

To the left is the top of the forward smokestack. At the bottom is the port Mk. 37 secondary-battery director, with its Mk. 25 radar antenna on top of it. Farther aft are the four portside Tomahawk ABLs, the nearest of which is in an elevated position.

In the foreground is the top of the *Wisconsin*'s forward smokestack, with a black cover over it. Farther aft, framed by the mainmast support structure, is the aft smokestack. Note the diagonal orientation of the four ABLs adjacent to the aft smokestack.

MUSEUM SHIP 121

The two forward port ABLs are viewed from alongside the forward smokestack. The closer ABL is elevated to its fixed angle for firing. The four forward ABLs were oriented facing inward, and they fired their missiles in that direction.

The forward port ABL of the *Wisconsin* is observed from a close perspective. Inside the elevated part of the launcher are four tubes, which held the Tomahawk cruise missiles. Next to this launcher is another ABL.

The aft smokestack and the four aft Tomahawk cruise missile ABLs are in view. These ABLs are arranged diagonally to the fore-and-aft centerline of the ship. They fired missiles toward their fronts. To the left is the UNREP outrigger.

Two of the Harpoon launchers are viewed close-up. The nearer launcher lacks the Mk. 141 launching tubes, while the other launcher is fitted with the tubes.

In a view taken from toward the rear of the starboard side of the superstructure, in the foreground is the forward starboard Harpoon antiship missile launcher, equipped with four Mk. 141 ceramic-armor launching tubes. Above the front of the superstructure are the towering TACAN antenna and the SPS-49 radar antenna.

The US Marine Corps emblem is emblazoned on the front of the armored shield of one of the *Wisconsin*'s twin 5-inch/38-caliber gun mounts, in honor of the Marine gunners who operated these mounts. On each Iowa-class battleship, one of these twin mounts was manned by a USMC crew.

MUSEUM SHIP 123

The interior of the pilothouse, also called the navigating bridge, of the *Wisconsin* is seen from the starboard side. Extensive windows gave the crew excellent protection from the elements.

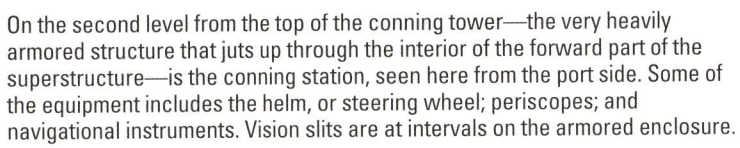

On the second level from the top of the conning tower—the very heavily armored structure that juts up through the interior of the forward part of the superstructure—is the conning station, seen here from the port side. Some of the equipment includes the helm, or steering wheel; periscopes; and navigational instruments. Vision slits are at intervals on the armored enclosure.

Running for 256 feet along the centerline of the third deck of the *Wisconsin* is the 6-foot-wide corridor nicknamed "Broadway." It constitutes the longest continuous passageway in the ship. Below the ceiling is a monorail, for shuttling heavy equipment and ammunition back and forth.

The dome-shaped object in the foreground of this photo taken in fireroom number 1 is the steam drum near the top of a Babcock & Wilcox boiler. To the left are handwheels for controlling valves.

Valve handwheels, gears, and insulated pipes in *Wisconsin*'s fireroom number 1 are displayed.

To the left is a boiler in engine room number 1; steam pipes are in the background.

The *Wisconsin* has four engine rooms, each of which is equipped with a low-pressure turbine, a high-pressure turbine, a reduction gear, turbogenerators, and other machinery. Engine room number 1 is depicted here, featuring a turbine with a diagram of the propulsion system projected on it.

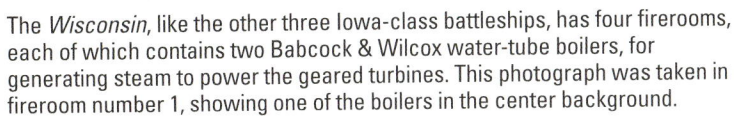

The *Wisconsin*, like the other three Iowa-class battleships, has four firerooms, each of which contains two Babcock & Wilcox water-tube boilers, for generating steam to power the geared turbines. This photograph was taken in fireroom number 1, showing one of the boilers in the center background.

The number 1 propeller shaft is shown at the point that it exits the reduction gears. The red-and-white stripes are painted on the shaft so that the engineering gang can see if the shaft is turning. If it were painted a solid color, it would be much more difficult to note rotation, especially if the lighting were damaged.

Wisconsin's turret 3 is the focus of this view taken from the starboard side of the aviation service center (*left*). During the latter part of the *Wisconsin*'s active service, it was configured for helicopters to land and take off from its fantail. On the rear of the superstructure directly above the turret roof is the helicopter control station, atop which is the aft Mk. 37 secondary-battery director.